Freedom From Fear, Anxiety, and Panic Attacks

Freedom From Fear, Anxiety, and Panic Attacks

by
David Crank

Harrison House
Tulsa, Oklahoma

Freedom From Fear, Anxiety, and Panic Attacks
ISBN 0-89274-926-1
Copyright © 1995 by David Crank
1416 Larkin Williams Road
St. Louis, MO 63026

Contents

Foreword

It is with a warm sense of thanksgiving that I write this foreword to *Freedom from Fear, Anxiety, and Panic Attacks*, my friend, David Crank's, new book.

I am thankful to the Lord, first of all, for David's courage to open the door for all of us to a subject that most preachers have been unwilling or unable to write about. David's courage to write on this subject, which has been so infrequently preached or talked about, is a great testimony to his desire to see you free from your fears, anxieties and panic attacks.

With his forthright testimonial style, David writes a book that is applicable to your everyday life and reads almost like a devotional. As you read the book chapter by chapter you will no doubt have the same experience that I did. In each chapter there was a nugget of truth that truly stayed with me throughout the remainder of my day.

Secondly, I am thankful that David is a Word-oriented preacher. Truly, man does not live by bread alone, but by every word that comes out of the mouth of God. The book you are about to read will cause you to have a "Word explosion" in your inner man. As you read, let me encourage you to ask the Holy Spirit to let the Word that David Crank so boldly shares come alive in your heart. That Word will set you free!

And thirdly, I have no doubt that *Freedom from Fear, Anxiety, and Panic Attacks* is going to release great healing to the body of Christ. My inner man was so greatly encouraged while reading this book, not only because of the blessing I received, but also because I am convinced that whoever reads this book is going to experience a deliverance that will last and that can be given to others.

I thank the Lord for giving David the courage to bring a rhema word to a subject that has been so long neglected and yet greatly needed. I am believing as you read, the Holy Spirit is going to set you free from your fears and anxieties.

God bless you is my prayer,

Larry Lea

Introduction

Many times we get ourselves in a mess — physically, emotionally and mentally — because we violate the laws of nature, the laws God set into motion when He created the universe.

At times I have gone through horrendous trials, which were not from God or the devil, but because I violated my own body. Although the devil will always try to take advantage of any situation when we are down, I could not blame him for my own stupidity!

Through the years I had established some very destructive habits where my health was concerned. I used to pray and read the Bible until two o'clock in the morning. That would be all right if I stayed in bed the next morning, but I did not. I always got up early, running on four or five hours of sleep a day for years.

We were travelling ministers for many years, and during that time I went day and night with little rest. There were times when I would preach two meetings a day (held in a tent) for eight straight weeks. I had to ring water out of my shirt because of heat and humidity outside. That would have been okay if I had been balancing out all this work with enough rest and relaxation, but I was not.

I could get by with a constantly hectic schedule while I was younger, but as the years passed and I grew older, I began to wear down. As a result, I injured my body, specifically my central nervous system, and this brought on the worst time of my life.

That horrendous period of my life is what this book is all about. I've written it to help others who are facing the same nightmare I faced, a nightmare where suddenly your entire being is gripped with terror, your body feels like it is dying, and your whole life is out of control. Basically, you feel like you have died and gone to hell — yet you are still alive.

What I am beginning to describe here is a panic attack, which is probably the worst thing I have ever experienced. When I first started having panic attacks, I didn't know what was happening to me. All I knew was that they were terrible and I wanted them to stop. Through God's help, I overcame them, and I am here to tell you that if you are suffering from any kind of fear, anxiety, or panic, you can too.

Most important, if you follow the principles of what I call *Holy Ghost Psychiatry*, you will probably never have to deal with a panic attack! As you take these principles to heart and begin to practice them, you will become stronger physically and mentally. Worry and the cares of this world will find no dwelling place in your mind. You will begin to speak and live by the wisdom that comes from possessing the mind of Christ — free from all fear, anxiety, and panic attacks.

We have the mind of Christ, the Messiah, and do hold the thoughts (feelings and purposes) of His heart.
First Corinthians 2:16

David Crank

1
Panic Attack!

In the late eighties, I literally walked through a measure of hell. There was even a time when thoughts of killing myself came to my mind. My mother had just died a tragic death after being bitten by a brown recluse spider. Then shortly after her death my father also died suddenly. On top of the intense grieving I was going through, several television ministries were found in scandal. Being on television myself, that brought incredible pressure.

I have already told you how I had abused my body for years. Therefore, when all these traumatic events happened at the same time, I was overwhelmed by worry and fear. Suddenly reality as I had known it was swept away as I began having panic attacks, one after the other. I couldn't sleep, eat, or sit still. My thoughts were like daggers of fear and so out of control that I could barely read God's Word or pray. I felt like I was trapped in darkness and would never be right again.

I have a service revolver from when I was a police officer for many years in St. Louis County. When I left the Police Department to go into full-time ministry, they presented me with my off-duty revolver. I've kept it loaded and stored above my bed in case we had an intruder at night. As the panic attacks grew worse and worse, the enemy introduced the thought, "You ought to get that gun and just end it all." The Word of God rose up in me, however, and I did not in any way yield to that thought. I knew it was a demon, tempting me to hurt myself. Satan always comes to steal, kill and destroy. (See John 10:10.)

Natural Medicine and Spiritual Medicine

In desperation I went to a medical doctor who had given me annual physical check-ups. He had never seen me sick, and I had never had an operation or been in a hospital. When any symptoms of illness tried to get ahold of me, I believed God's promise of healing and got free of them every time. But now I went to this doctor in the height of what they call a classic burnout or nervous breakdown.

He listened quietly as I talked to him about what I was going through, and then he began to speak very kindly and gently. Although psychology was not his specialty, he sensed I needed that. Later he told me that he perceived I was really on the edge of a total collapse that day, and if it had been anybody else, he would have put me in the hospital. But he knew I had a lot of family support, and I had taken a close minister friend of mine with me who would help me through the process of recovery.

The doctor prescribed some medication to help me sleep. My thoughts were so out of control, and the panic attacks were coming so fast and often, that I wasn't able to rest. If your mind won't shut down, you won't sleep. It's like a gyroscope in an airplane that keeps whirling and whirling. By the time I saw the doctor, I could not sleep at all. I was up day and night. Now you can imagine what that would do to a person who was perfectly healthy, but to someone whose nervous system had been damaged year after year, not getting any sleep was disastrous and made the panic attacks worse.

For a period of time in the beginning I was on heavy medication. Because I had always been opposed to any kind of medication, this was very hard for me. Now as I look back on it, I know it was an area of pride in my life. My thinking was, "I don't have to be on medication. I believe there's a *higher* level of medication." That's true. The Word of God is a higher level of medication, but in my state of mind, I was not able to take God's medicine!

For years before all this happened, my habit was not to take God's medicine as I went to sleep. Instead, I chose to lay in bed at night for hours and think about problems and try to find answers to those problems — and anything else that I could find to worry about. Many times the Holy Spirit gently tried to tell me that what I was doing was wrong. I had promptings, urgings, and even the actual authoritative voice of the Holy Ghost say, "Now is the time to go to sleep." But I ignored Him and consequently I injured myself.

Repeatedly from a young age I had not chosen the higher level of medication. I chose to be disobedient to the unctions and urgings and promptings of the Holy Ghost. Instead of praising God, calming my mind with His Word, and casting all my cares on the Lord every night, I had chosen to meditate on fears and anxious thoughts.

There are two worlds, the supernatural and the natural. There is the spiritual world and the physical world. The spiritual world is the higher world, because it existed before the physical world. The spiritual world is the parent and the physical world is the child.

In the same way, there is spiritual medicine and natural medicine. The spiritual medicine is God's Word. Proverbs 4:20-22 (KJV) says, **My son, attend to my words; incline thine ear unto my sayings. Let them not depart from thine eyes; Keep them in the midst of thine heart. For they are life unto those that find them, and health to all their flesh.**

If a believer is not taking God's medicine, you can count on the fact that eventually they will have to take natural medicine! When you go your own way as long as I did, every night for years, then you will eventually destroy your sense of well-being and nervous system.

By the time I started having panic attacks, I needed the natural medicine to calm myself enough to be able to take the spiritual medicine, which is God's Word. Until my thoughts were brought under control, I could barely read the print in my Bible, not to mention meditate on what was there.

When I did not want to take the natural medicine because of my pride, the Holy Spirit on the inside of me said, "Son, go the natural way. Medicine and faith can be mixed." Then He directed me to James 1:17 (KJV), **Every good gift and every perfect gift is from above, and cometh down from the Father of lights, with whom is no variableness, neither shadow of turning.** Doctors (most of them) are good, and medicine (used correctly) is also good. Only God is perfect, but He has given us many good things to help us.

Both my doctor and the medication he prescribed helped me overcome this horrible ordeal. I have humbly come to realize that God created doctors and medicine and they can be a blessing to our lives. The truth is, if it wasn't for doctors and medication, most Christians would be dead! So I encourage you to seek a godly physician and be led by the Spirit of God. Do not be antagonistic toward doctors. They want you to be well too!

All the time I was taking natural medication, I was taking God's medication. I was heavily medicating myself with the Word of God, memorizing and meditating on scripture after scripture. Eventually I was able to begin decreasing the natural medication as the spiritual medication began to bring health to my flesh. This was a very gradual process, however. As my soul was restored by taking in the Word of God and doing it, that spiritual medicine began to take over more and more and I needed the natural medicine less and less. Finally, the day came when I was able to stop taking the natural medicine altogether.

My doctor had also recommended a psychiatrist to me, but I didn't feel the need for one. I knew the root of my problem was that I had been disobedient to the Word of God regarding worry. I had not trained myself to relax and cast all my cares upon the Lord. I worked long hours, never took vacations, and rarely took a day off. I had abused the good health God had given me and violated the temple of the Holy Ghost, my body.

I also knew I had many family members and brothers and sisters in the Lord to talk to. But if you feel the need for a psychologist or psychiatrist, I don't believe God is against this. There are many good, godly mental health specialists who can help you. Don't let some kind of religious pride get in the way of your getting healed!

What Is a Panic Attack?

Sometimes you can tell what something is by saying what it is not. A panic attack is not just a bad day. It is not just being depressed. It is not a bad mental attitude you can easily shake. It is stark, dark, bizarre, horrendous, horrible fear. I don't know all the pathology of it. Doctors and experts might give you a more technical definition, but having experienced a panic attack, the best way to describe it is just sheer, unadulterated terror. You don't know what you are afraid of or what is happening to you. All you know is that you are terrified.

I did not know what was happening to me in the winter of 1988 when I experienced my first panic attack. I had no idea what it was, which increased the fear because it was unknown to me. It can be accompanied by many different physical symptoms, such as dryness of the mouth, heart palpitations or increase in heartrate, nausea, diarrhea, chills, hot flashes, trembling, etc. Any of these symptoms would not be so bad, but when they are connected with panic you think you are dying.

You know a panic attack is beginning when you start to experience great sensations of fear, confusion, and difficulty controlling your own thoughts. It's hard to reason and control your mind, and then you anticipate some or all of the above-mentioned physical symptoms which can occur during a panic attack.

There is a natural pathology to a panic attack, which a psychologist or specialist could describe, but as believers we can understand how demon spirits are involved also. At a time of weakness or crisis, they will introduce thoughts of fear and panic to try to incite a panic attack.

For example, I prayed for a girl who was experiencing tremendous chronic mental problems and panic attacks. She was trembling before me as she said, "Something keeps telling me that I've committed the unpardonable sin." I said, "You don't know how many people I've counseled with who have told me the exact same thing in an emotional battle."

The devil is so lousy and mean, he'll take advantage of any situation and tell you that you committed the unpardonable sin. That's a lie! First, if you are afraid you've committed the unpardonable sin, you haven't committed it! If you had you wouldn't care, because you would have totally rejected God.

This is another reason why studying the Word is so important. We have to understand how the enemy operates. It's not enough to know that he is out to get us; we must learn how he does it so we can neutralize him. We can have total confidence that through the name of Jesus he can be totally defeated.

How Do You Get Out of This?

Sometimes in feeling a panic attack coming on, I can remember almost forgetting to breathe. I would hold my breath and not realize it. One thing the Spirit of God instructed me to begin to do was to totally relax my body by lying still and breathing deeply. Later on a television show I heard a medical person say that when you begin to feel panicky you should begin to breathe deeply. I thought of it this way: Breathe in the power of the Holy Spirit, breathe out problems. Breathe in God's Word, breathe out worry. Cast all care on God.

Whatever thought or event it is that triggered the panic attack, whether finances, marriage, children, or something else, now is not the time to think about it! You have to recognize that just a thought of something stressful can increase the hold a panic attack has on you. So cast down every thought that involves fear or worry or stress immediately and turn your thoughts to Jesus.

For many years I worked on getting a private pilot's license. I remember when I got enough hours to solo. The instructor got out of the airplane and told me to take off. I'll never forget that day! I pushed down the yoke, gave it full power, lifted off, and thoughts flooded my mind, "Oh my God! The devil has got you right where he wants you. You're going to kill yourself."

But I controlled those thoughts. I pushed down that fear and controlled my mind. I had to control my mind or else I would have forgotten the crosswind leg, the downward leg, the final approach, and all those things I had to memorize to get that airplane safely back on the ground!

After I soloed, the instructor told me there were three things I always needed to remember in flying an airplane: communicate, navigate, and aviate. He said, "If you're ever up there and you get in trouble, if you can, communicate with somebody at the tower. But while the tower is helping you and giving you instructions on how to navigate, don't forget to aviate! Don't stop flying the airplane!"

He said there had been students who crashed because they were so intent on listening to the communication with the tower and trying to navigate themselves back to the airport, they forgot to aviate. In the same way, when a panic attack strikes, don't forget to breathe!

Control your thoughts by focusing on the Lord and, if necessary, taking medication according to your doctor's instructions. Forget about the problems. Forget about the situation that got you into this present state. Begin saying what the Word says: Everything is going to be alright! Everything is going to be fine. Everything is going to be wonderful.

Throughout this book I give you scriptures God gave me in the height of this battle. Every chapter deals with a different area of your life where, if you do not keep your mind on God's Word concerning it, you can become fearful and stressed and eventually fall into a panic attack.

The following chapters outline the principles of Holy Ghost Psychiatry. If you are suffering from intense fear, anxiety, or panic attacks, the devil and your uneducated brain will tell you that you're never going to be the same, you'll never come out of this. But I came out of it and you will too!

Practicing Holy Ghost Psychiatry works! As you read through each chapter, put these principles to work in your life and see what happens. I am beautifully and wonderfully healed and you can be also.

2
Thinking God's Thoughts

The Spirit of the Lord spoke to me one day and told me that Satan is planning an all-out attack against the minds of believers as never before. This is because the arena of the mind is where victory or defeat takes place. The good news is that Satan does not have enough darkness to extinguish light. The Bible says believers are light and salt in the earth.

> You are the salt of the earth, but if salt has lost its taste — its strength, its quality — how can its saltness be restored? It is not good for anything any longer but to be thrown out and trodden underfoot by men.
>
> You are the light of the world. A city set on a hill cannot be hid. Nor do men light a lamp and put it under a peck-measure, but on a lampstand, and it gives light to all in the house.
>
> Let your light so shine before men that they may see your moral excellence and your praiseworthy, noble and good deeds, and recognize and honor and praise and glorify your Father Who is in heaven.
>
> Matthew 5:13-16

God's precious people are the only thing that keeps the world from spoiling, so of course the great spoiler, the devil, would like to destroy us. He knows that if he can capture our minds, he can defeat us and spoil our lives. This will keep our light from shining, and that's why it is so important to guard our minds.

Many Christians are reluctant to discuss the mind because certain cults and doctrines of devils have focused on this area. But the Bible, which is the foundation of Holy

Ghost Psychiatry, has a lot to say about the mind. Philippians 2:5 says, **Let this same attitude and purpose and [humble] mind be in you which was in Christ Jesus: [Let Him be your example in humility].**

Romans 12:2 (KJV) says, **Be not conformed to this world: but be ye transformed by the renewing of your mind, that ye may prove what is that good, and acceptable, and perfect will of God.**

The Amplified Bible says, **Do not be conformed to this world — this age — [fashioned after and adapted to its external, superficial customs. But be transformed (changed) by the [entire] renewal of your mind — by its new ideals and its new attitude — so that you may prove [for yourselves] what is the good and acceptable and perfect will of God, even the thing which is good and acceptable and perfect [in His sight for you].**

Since Satan constantly bombards the mind with negative, put-down, disparaging thoughts, you need to know what God has to say about the mind. Knowing the promises of God's Word concerning soundness of mind will keep you in **the day of trouble** (Ps. 59:16). This phrase, "the day of trouble," refers to times when Satan and his imps are assigned to put negative thoughts in your mind. These thoughts are more intense at certain times than at others.

The devil will begin to raise questions about potential problems or harmful situations that might arise. His motive is to keep you anxious, fretting about tomorrow or ten minutes from now or ten weeks from now or years in the future. To combat these attacks, you must renew your mind — every day — by feeding and meditating upon God's Word.

You must live life a day at a time. Anxiety is being anxious about that which is ahead, whether a year ahead, a month ahead, two days ahead, or tomorrow. You break a law of God when you become anxious about what's going to happen in the future, because He gives you strength for today and has already provided for tomorrow.

This precedent was illustrated most clearly in the Old Testament when He fed the children of Israel manna *daily*. If they got anxious about tomorrow and kept more manna than they needed for that day, the next morning it had maggots in it! God does not work that way. You have got to live and trust God for today. *Today* is the day of salvation. Learning this has changed my life!

Manna for the believer is the Word of God. Each day we are to get up and take in God's Word to see us through that day victoriously. Jesus said, "Give us this day our daily bread" (Matt. 6:11). I have learned through the years that in order to live victoriously in an area of my life, I have to get into a daily consumption of that area of the Word.

For example, to prosper financially, I needed to find, study, and meditate on scriptures on finances. My parents had always had financial problems, and they lived in poverty all their life. They taught us to pay our bills, but that was it. They never taught us to tithe or give to the Lord, and I was very illiterate concerning giving. As a result, my first few years traveling full-time across the country on the evangelistic field were some of our hardest times financially.

It wasn't long before I made a decision to study from Genesis to Revelation and find out what the Bible says about finances. I committed myself to develop a fortress of God's Word concerning finances around me, and I did. The years have come and gone, and not only do I have awesome faith concerning finances, but we are totally blessed.

Brother Kenneth E. Hagin made the statement once, "Thinking faith thoughts and speaking faith words will lead the heart out of defeat into victory every time. Thoughts may come and thoughts may persist in staying, but thoughts not spoken or acted upon will die unborn." Those words worked mightily in my life when I fought the battle against panic attacks.

You can slowly but surely build a fortress of God's Word in your mind and around your emotions and nervous system, a fortress that will keep worry and fear from getting ahold of your heart again. You will think God's thoughts and speak His words and be victorious in the most trying circumstances.

Over the years I've memorized many scriptures, but I'm always adding new ones to my mindbank. Through the battle with panic attacks, I memorized scriptures mostly out of the *Amplified Bible*. God knows what's in every translation of the Bible, and He'll lead you to the translation that will help you the most for what you are going through at the time.

I would not just think these scriptures, but I would also speak them to myself. The Bible says to talk to yourself in psalms and hymns and spiritual songs (Eph. 5:19), so I would speak God's Word to myself. **The Lord is my Shepherd, he restores my soul.**

Many times I addressed myself by name. Second Corinthians 2:14 says, **Now thanks be to God which always causes us to triumph in Christ,** so I would say, "David, you're going to triumph in this. You're going to come out of this, David. Everything's going to be alright. Everything's going to be okay." This really helped me.

Another part of my healing from panic attacks was to train myself to think differently when I went to bed at night. When it's time to go to sleep, I calm my mind. If I'm having a difficult time settling down, I praise the Lord. "Thank you Jesus. I praise you Jesus. I bless you Lord."

By thinking and speaking God's Word instead of entertaining thoughts of worry and fear, you are restoring your own soul. Your soul is your mind (physical brain), your will, and your emotions, and you are restoring them by speaking the Word of God. Although building a fortress of God's Word around you happens a brick at a time, over a period of time a mighty wall constructed of knowledge and faith will be a part of your thinking, speaking, and doing.

God has made you the custodian of your mind, and Jesus admonished you to take heed what those two appendages on the sides of your cranial cavity hear — not only from people, but from the devil. Get rid of all worry thoughts, anxious thoughts, and foreboding thoughts.

Second Timothy 1:7 (KJV) says, **God hath not given us the spirit of fear; but of power, and of love, and of a sound mind.** *The Amplified Bible* says, **God did not give us a spirit of timidity — of cowardice, of craven and cringing and fawning fear — but [He has given us a spirit] of power and of love and of calm and well-balanced mind and discipline and self-control.**

So think like God and speak like God. Then you will act like God and, when the day is done, rest in His peace.

3

Seeking God's Kingdom First

The entire third chapter of the epistle to the Colossians has to do with having a sound mind and is a great source for the principles of Holy Ghost Psychiatry. By examining these principles we can learn how to build a spiritual wall which will protect us from Satan's weapons of anxiety, worry, care, and concern.

If you were protecting your property from a possible flood, you would build a wall with sandbags to hold back the flood waters. But unlike sandbags which can be moved or overcome, God's Word is immovable and forever settled in heaven (Psalm 119:89).

If then you have been raised with Christ [to a new life, thus sharing His resurrection from the dead], aim at and seek the [rich, eternal treasures] that are above, where Christ is, seated at the right hand of God.

Colossians 3:1

The King James Version says, **If ye then be risen with Christ, seek those things which are above, where Christ sitteth on the right hand of God.**

This verse does not say we are not to have anything on this earth. God wants to bless us with abundant life and material things. But for peace of mind, we are not to *seek* material things. We are to *seek* the things "which are above."

Our number one priority is found in Matthew 6:31-34. Jesus said:

Therefore do not worry and be anxious, saying, What are we going to have to eat? or, What are we going to have to drink? or, What are we going to have to wear?

27

For the Gentiles (heathen) wish for and crave and diligently seek all these things; and your heavenly Father knows well that you need them all.

But seek for (aim at and strive after) first of all His kingdom, and His righteousness (His way of doing and being right), and then all these things taken together will be given you besides.

So do not worry or be anxious about tomorrow, for tomorrow will have worries and anxieties of its own. Sufficient for each day is its own trouble.

God is not against you having material things, but He is against you seeking them more than you seek Him. If you seek Him, you wil not worry about finances and having things. You will have peace.

Then shall you delight yourself in the Lord, and I will make you to ride on the high places of the earth, and I will feed you with the heritage [promised for you] of Jacob your father; for the mouth of the Lord has spoken it.

Isaiah 58:14

If you are seeking "things," your mind will not stay in peace. Satan will steal your peace, the most important commodity you can ever get your hot little hands on! But if you want **to ride on the high places**, then **delight yourself in the Lord.**

Holy Ghost Psychiatry requires that you set your mind on things above rather than on natural things of the earth. **Seeking those things which are above** includes seeking the fruit of the Holy Spirit, living right, praying, reading the Bible, and helping wounded, needy people.

As you pursue the things which are above, those things associated with your spiritual maturity, God will take care of the natural realm. Your material problems will begin to fade away and God will bless you!

And set your minds and keep them set on what is above — the higher things — not on the things that are on the earth.

For [as far as this world is concerned] you have died, and your [new, real] life is hidden with Christ in God.

When Christ Who is our life appears, then you also will appear with Him in [the splendor of His] glory.

Colossians 3:2-4

4

Surrendering Your Body

So kill (deaden, deprive of power) the evil desire lurking in your members — those animal impulses.

Colossians 3:5

Man is a spirit being. That is the only thing which separates us from animals. I do not believe that a horse has a spirit. If someone shot your horse, I do not believe his little horsey spirit would fly on up to heaven! Animals have souls (minds, wills, and emotions) and "personalities" just like people do, but they do not have spirits. The only reference in the Bible of God breathing His Spirit into any living thing is found in Genesis 2:7, which refers only to man: **Then the Lord God formed man from the dust of the ground** *and breathed into his nostrils the breath or spirit of life;* **and man became a living being.**

Even though God has given us a spirit, we human beings still have animalistic tendencies motivated by our physical bodies and appetites. Have you ever seen hogs shove and fight each other when food is thrown into their pen? This is a good example of animalism. All human beings have these impulses, and we choose to act upon them or not.

You will never have peace of mind if you give your body free course. Paul, referring to disciplining his body (not specifically to its animalistic impulses) said:

But [like a boxer] I buffet my body — handle it roughly, discipline it by hardships — and subdue it, for fear that after proclaiming to others the Gospel and

31

things pertaining to it, I myself should become unfit [not stand the test — be unapproved and rejected as a counterfeit.]

First Corinthians 9:27

Certain verses in the Bible cannot be understood by your mind (brain) or your body. And of course, the devil cannot understand them. They must be discerned by your spirit. One such verse is Matthew 10:39:

Whoever finds his [lower] life will lose it [the higher life], and whoever loses his [lower] life on My account will find [the higher life].

Another example is Luke 6:38 (KJV):

Give, and it shall be given unto you; good measure, pressed down, and shaken together, and running over, shall men give into your bosom. For with the same measure that ye mete withal it shall be measured to you again.

The flesh is greedy. Did you know that greed will actually prevent a person from having money? Greed says, "Hold onto every dollar you've got," but God is a giver and we are to imitate Him. His Word says that the more you give, the more you will receive. (See 2 Cor. 9:6.)

Psalm 39:6 says, **Each one heaps up riches, not knowing who will gather them.** Actually, rich men are heaping up riches in these last days for those who are heirs of righteousness (Prov. 13:22). Though they think they are getting it for themselves, they are heaping it up for us!

Being greedy with money is almost like not having any money. Certainly the Bible teaches us to be good stewards of all God gives us, to be frugal and to walk in wisdom. Nevertheless, the Bible does not teach us to be stingy and greedy to the point that we resent buying anything.

Some people are so tight that they refuse to give tithes or offerings to God. They may think they are saving money, but actually they are cutting themselves off from God and the blessings that He wants to give them. It is God Who causes men to give into your bosom and Who causes you to reap in like measure to what you have sown.

Another verse which runs contrary to man's carnal nature deals with loving your enemies and those who persecute you.

> But I tell you, love your enemies and pray for those who persecute you, to show that you are the children of your Father who is in heaven; for he makes his sun rise on the wicked and on the good, and makes the rain fall upon the upright and the wrongdoers [alike]. For if you love those who love you, what reward can you have? Do not even the tax collectors do that? And if you greet only your brethren, what more than others are you doing? Do not even the Gentiles (the heathen) do that? You, therefore, must be perfect [growing into complete maturity of godliness in mind and character, having reached the proper height of virtue and integrity], as your heavenly Father is perfect.
>
> Matthew 5:44-48

It is common for people to follow their animalistic instincts until they have learned to be led by the Spirit of God. Our five-year-old son, Anthony, is the sweetest little jewel God ever put on this earth. Still, he has been known to have temper tantrums at times. Though he is so sweet, he is so human! Sometimes his little animalistic body takes over. Many people, without the rule and reign of the Holy Spirit, have wanted to knock their enemies into the next county! But you cannot follow animalistic impulses and expect to have peace of mind.

In Christ You Are A New Creation

In the past I have heard teachers on radio and television state that people have a "dualistic personality," that we humans have both the nature of God and the nature of the devil. But the scriptures teach otherwise: **Therefore if any** man be in Christ, he is a *new creature*: old things are passed away; behold, all things are become new (2 Cor. 5:17, KJV).

Jesus spoke to Nicodemus about how to take on the new nature.

> There was a man of the Pharisees, named Nicodemus, a ruler of the Jews:
>
> The same came to Jesus by night, and said unto him, Rabbi, we know that thou art a teacher come from God: for no man can do these miracles that thou doest, except God be with him.
>
> Jesus answered and said unto him, Verily, verily, I say unto thee, Except a man be born again, he cannot see the kingdom of God.
>
> Nicodemus saith unto him, How can a man be born when he is old? can he enter the second time into his mother's womb, and be born?
>
> Jesus answered, Verily, verily, I say unto thee, Except a man be born of water and of the Spirit, he cannot enter into the kingdom of God.
>
> That which is born of the flesh is flesh; and that which is born of the Spirit is spirit.
>
> Marvel not that I said unto thee, Ye must be born again.
>
> John 3:1-7 (KJV)

Nicodemus was saying, "I don't understand this new birth. You say I must be born again. How do I go back into my mama's womb? I am forty years old and weigh 210 pounds." But Jesus responded, **That which is born of flesh is flesh, and that which is born of Spirit is spirit.** A born-again believer does not have a dual nature. They take on God's nature in place of their old nature. Still, they have to choose to follow after their new Christlike nature instead of the old Satanlike nature.

Have you ever had someone cut in front of you in traffic? Have you noticed that something other than God's nature can take over instantly if you let it? Is that your "dual nature"? No, that is your flesh! It is calling you to act in line with your old nature instead of your new nature.

Dominating Your Flesh With the Word

When you are born again, you have the nature of God. **The love of God is shed abroad in our hearts by the Holy Spirit which is given to us** (Rom. 5:5, KJV). First John 2:16 says,

> **For all that is in the world, the lust of the flesh [craving for sensual gratification], and the lust of the eyes [greedy longings of the mind] and the pride of life [assurance in one's own resources or in the stability of earthly things] — these do not come from the Father but are from the world [itself].**

You do not have a dual nature. You are the righteousness of God in Christ. You are a spirit being, but you dwell in flesh and your flesh has never been saved. Scripture says to renew your mind with the Word of God. James 1:21 says,

> **So get rid of all uncleanness and the rampant outgrowth of wickedness, and in a humble (gentle, modest) spirit receive and welcome the Word which implanted and rooted [in your hearts] contains the power to save your souls.**

Until your mind and body are brought into subjection to God's Word, you will still think some carnal thoughts. As far as your spirit is concerned, however, at the new birth your human spirit is recreated and you are instantly as righteous as you will ever be. You are as perfect as you will ever be, even though nothing happens to your body or to your brain. Therefore you must control the flesh if you are to have peace of mind and be free from fear, anxiety, and guilt.

> **So kill (deaden, deprive of power) the evil desire lurking in your members — those animal impulses and**

35

all that is earthly in you that is employed in sin: sexual vice, impurity, sensual appetites, unholy desires, and all greed and covetousness, for that is idolatry [the deifying of self and other created things instead of God].

Colossians 3:5

The body is very impulsive and will suddenly push you to do certain things you know you should not do. But when you are dominated by God's Spirit and by His Word, you will have control over your body. **It is on account of these [very sins] that the [holy] anger of God is ever coming upon the sons of disobedience (those who are obstinately opposed to the divine will (Col. 3:6).**

Paul is talking about the sins that he previously listed in verse 5: **sexual vice, impurity, sensual appetites, unholy desires, and all greed and covetousness.** And as to those opposed to God's divine will, Paul says, these are the ones **among whom you also once walked, when you were living in and addicted to [such] practices (Col. 3:7).**

When your fleshly, carnal nature is dominated by the Word of God, you will experience love and peace and joy, but if you allow your flesh to dominate, your peace will go right out the window! This is Holy Ghost Psychiatry! You will never have peace of mind until you deprive your animalistic body of power. You have to respond to the impulses of the flesh by saying, "No, you don't!" And then surrender your body totally to the Spirit of God.

5

Getting Rid of Fleshly Attributes

But now put away and rid yourselves [completely] of all these things: anger, rage, bad feeling toward others, curses and slander, and foulmouthed abuse and shameful utterances from your lips!

Colossians 3:8

It takes time to rid yourself of fleshly attributes. If you want God's psychiatry for peace of mind, then rid yourself completely of all **anger, rage, bad feeling toward others, curses and slander, and foulmouthed abuse and shameful utterances from your lips!**

When the Word is sown, Satan comes immediately to steal the Word. He will try to get some anger in your life, so be watchful and sober. It is easy to be angry, but Holy Ghost Psychiatry will help you rid yourself of this fleshly attribute. Proverbs 15:1 says, **A soft answer turns away wrath; but grievous words stir up anger.**

I cannot tell you how much this word has helped my household. Years ago my wife, Sharon, started practicing how to respond with a soft answer, and she motivated me to do the same. We both practice it now. It is bad enough if one person uses "grievous words," but if both husband and wife bellow, then it is pandemonium in the penthouse!

Many people blame their anger on external factors, such as their national origin or their red hair. That does not have anything to do with it. It is just flesh! Philippians 4:13 (KJV) says, **I can do all things through Christ which strengtheneth me,** and that means we can control anger by drawing on the power of the Holy Spirit within us.

Jesus was a robust, strong man, not weak or wimpy. I believe He was tempted to act in the flesh at times because Scripture says, **For we have not an high priest which cannot be touched with the feeling of our infirmities; but was in all points tempted like as we are, yet without sin** (Heb. 4:15 (KJV). When Jesus was spit upon, His beard was plucked out, and His enemies said, "If You're the King of the Jews, then prophesy and call angels," I believe He was tempted to be angry.

When you hear someone slandering, cursing, or abusing with a foul mouth, you will know automatically they are in the wrong spirit. If the words are abusive, foulmouthed, or slanderous, the one speaking has a nasty spirit. When you do these things, you open the door to the devil. You invite him in. The devil is the god of these things.

There are people who open the door to the devil and then say, "Why did God do this to me? Why did God let this happen?" God did not do anything. *They* let it happen with the words of their own mouth. *But you can make a decision to stay in a sweet spirit.*

Put Away Lying

Do not lie to one another, for you have stripped off the old (unregenerate) self with its evil practices, and have clothed yourselves with the new [spiritual self], which is (ever in the process of being) renewed and remolded into (fuller and more perfect knowledge upon) knowledge after the image (the likeness) of Him who created it.

Colossians 3:9,10

Your word ought to be your bond. That is integrity. Lying will open the door to the devil to torment you. I am amazed that there are so many Christians who still lie like dogs! Unbelievable!

Integrity includes respect for God. You should get to church on time. You would not think of being late if you had to go before the Board of Directors of a major corporation. That would be disrespectful. Neither should we walk into the counsel of God late. People who do not honor God and the things of God as they should wonder why calamity comes like a whirlwind. Actually they are just reaping what they have sown.

We are to walk in honesty. This means paying your bills — on time. This means eliminating any degree of deception, which is just another form of lying. What is in the world will get in the body of Christ if we are not careful.

No Distinctions of Race or Culture in Christ

[In this new creation all distinctions vanish]; there is no room for and there can be neither Greek nor Jew, circumcised nor uncircumcised, [nor difference between nations whether alien] barbarians, or Scythinans [who are the most savage of all], nor slave or free man; but Christ is all and in all — everything and everywhere, to all men, without distinction of person.

Colossians 3:11

Do not let the devil beat you up with words. He will point out every weakness and character flaw. He is quick to say you will not be able to accomplish anything because of your race, lack of education, or because you have big ears and a big nose! But God says, let **all distinctions vanish.**

What if everyone was just alike? That would be horrible. I have heard my wife say as she looked for a new dress, "No, I don't want that one, I've seen fifteen of them." That means that even if she likes the dress, it is not unique. She wants something that is different. God wants each person to be different also. That is why He made various races and cultures.

Clothe Yourself with the Fruit of the Spirit

> Clothe yourselves therefore, as (God's own picked representatives,) His own chosen ones, [who are] purified and holy and well-beloved [by God Himself, by putting on behavior marked by] tenderhearted pity and mercy, kind feelings, a lowly opinion of yourselves, gentle ways [and] patience — which is tireless, long-suffering and has the power to endure whatever comes, with good temper.
>
> Colossians 3:12

Most people clothe themselves physically before starting their day. (You do not see too many stark-naked people, particularly in God's house!) In a similar fashion, you need to clothe yourself daily with the Word of God.

The Lord spoke to me one time and said, "How can you clothe yourself and put on something that you don't even have yet?" Then He told me to memorize the fruit of the Spirit as listed in Galatians 5:22,23.

When you commit to do something, God will help you. To simplify memorizing the fruit of the Spirit, He said, "Just divide the list into categories of three." When He said that, I realized how the fruit of the spirit fall into three general groups:

1. love, joy, peace;

2. longsuffering, gentleness, goodness; and

3. faith, meekness, temperance.

You will have an opportunity every single day, sometimes many times a day, to let the fruit of the Holy Spirit manifest from your spirit. Some people are angry one moment and the next they are not. They put on anger. But we can learn to put on longsuffering and gentleness. There are times when I am driving that I begin to get irritated with another driver. I will hear on the inside of me, "Be longsuffering and gentle." That is the Holy Ghost trying to keep me in the path of love, for love never fails.

Let Love Dominate Your Home

Wives, be subject to your husbands — subordinate and adapt yourselves to them — as is right and fitting and your proper duty in the Lord.

Husbands, love your wives — be affectionate and sympathetic with them — and do not be harsh or bitter or resentful toward them.

Colossians 3:18,19

People these days seem to think divorce is the answer to marriage problems. I even know of some divorces that took place because the wife thought her husband was interfering with her "ministry." But divorce is *not* the answer. That is just like trying to unscramble scrambled eggs. I suppose some people's lives are so scrambled they have no choice but to just go on and start again. Certainly our God is the God of a second chance, but it is much better (and God's desire) that we rid ourselves of selfishness, anger, and other fleshly attributes which detract from a solid marriage and family relationship.

Children, obey your parents in everything, for this is pleasing to the Lord.

Fathers, do not provoke or irritate or fret your children — do not be hard on them or harass them — lest they become discouraged and sullen and morose and feel inferior and frustrated; do not break their spirit.

Colossians 3:20,21

You should discipline your children, because the Bible also says, **foolishness is bound in the heart of a child; but the rod of correction shall drive it far from him** (Prov. 22:15, KJV), but we are to discipline our children in love. We are not to harass them or ride them continually. This is another principle of Holy Ghost Psychiatry that will lead to peace of mind and peace in the home.

Ephesians 4:32 (KJV) says, **Be ye kind one to another, tenderhearted, forgiving one another, even as God for**

Christ's sake hath forgiven you. Keep your heart "tender." If I watch a cowboy movie and the good guy dies, I cry. (I try to hide my tears from Sharon because I tell her that I am John Wayne, Superman, and Batman all rolled into one!) I cry because I am tenderhearted.

> **[Put] on behavior marked by tenderhearted pity and mercy, kind feeling, a lowly opinion of yourselves, gentle ways, [and] patience — which is tireless and long-suffering, and has the power to endure whatever comes, with good temper.**
>
> **Colossians 3:12**

Do not expect that you can become gentle, tenderhearted, patient, and long-suffering instantly. One time when I was praying (actually, I was griping to God about some members of my congregation!) God told me in no uncertain terms, "Everyone will not come to that level of spiritual maturity. It's not that they can't, but everyone won't reach that level, so quit trying to push the truth of the Word of God. You just preach it. Set it before them, and some of them will come up a little higher. You think everybody ought to come to a certain level and do it by next Tuesday, but you've got to be gentle."

When I chose to be gentle and patient with my congregation, I got peace of mind. The Word of God is the wisdom of God, and if you violate wisdom, you will see troublesome days and little peace of mind.

Readily Pardoning

> **Be gentle and forbearing with one another and, if one has a difference (a grievance or complaint) against another, *readily pardoning* each other; even as the Lord has freely forgiven you, so must you also [forgive].**
>
> **Colossians 3:13**

The debt Jesus forgave you and me is much larger than any debt we will ever forgive here on earth. No one could ever pay the price for keeping you and me out of hell. That is the biggest debt that has ever occurred, and Jesus paid it in full. Though His body was put in the tomb, He went to hell, where He took our punishment for three days and three nights. He whipped the devil and then arose victorious so you and I could live in victory in every area of life.

It is so important that we do not hurt people. Even if they have done us wrong or stabbed us in the back, we are not to retaliate or attempt to get vengeance, but we are to walk on in God's love. He is the vengeance giver. Romans 12:19 says, **Vengeance is Mine, I will repay (requite), says the Lord.** Therefore, our attitude should be one of readily pardoning.

The devil can never get a foothold of bitterness in your soul if you will turn all your offenses and hurts over to the Lord and forgive. By living this way, you will rest peacefully at night and awake refreshed for the day.

6

Men's Hearts Failing
Them for Fear

Fear is such a horrible thing. There is nothing quite like it. Fear is actually perverted faith. Faith comes by hearing God's Word and what He says about a situation, but fear comes by hearing the devil's word and what he says about something. The devil will always try to get you into what is called clinical depression — which leads to anxiety disorders.

> And there will be signs in the sun and moon and stars; and upon the earth [there will be] distress (trouble and anguish) of nations in bewilderment and perplexity [without resources, left wanting, embarrassed, in doubt, not knowing which way to turn] at the roaring (the echo) of the tossing of the sea.
>
> Men swooning away or expiring with fear and dread and apprehension and expectation of the things that are coming on the world; for the [very] powers of the heavens will be shaken and caused to totter.
>
> And then they will see the Son of Man coming in a cloud with great (transcendent and overwhelming) power and [all His kingly] glory (majesty and splendor).
>
> Now when these things begin to occur, look up and lift up your heads, because your redemption (deliverance) is drawing near.
>
> Luke 21: 25-28

I certainly do not have to attempt to prove to you that men's hearts are failing them for fear because of the things that are happening on the earth. First John 4:18 (KJV) says, **There is no fear in love; but perfect love casteth out fear: because fear hath torment. He that feareth is not made perfect in love.**

The Amplified Bible says,

> **There is no fear in love [dread does not exist]; but full-grown (complete, perfect) love turns fear out of doors and expels every trace of terror! For fear brings with it the thought of punishment, and [so] he who is afraid has not reached the full maturity of love [is not yet grown into love's complete perfection].**

Sometimes I feel as though every type of fear that has ever been on this earth has tried to attack me at one time or another. It is running rampant in America today. You see fearful things on television and in movies all the time.

Satan can do psychological warfare in your mind, but he cannot take control of your mind unless you have a door open to him (which can happen if you are playing with sin). If Satan could control you with fear, he already would have done it.

During one of the world wars, some of our soldiers were tortured with a tactic called psychological warfare. One method was to tie prisoners down under some kind of a contraption which continually dripped water on their heads. You may be thinking, "That wouldn't bother me much," but it would after about seven days of constant torture. You would break down.

I went into the army at the height of the Vietnam War. One of the enemy's psychological warfare tactics then was to put a prisoner in a locker and leave him in the hot sun all day long. Even when we were being trained to endure this kind of torture, I saw strong young men come apart from the pressure.

Similarly, if Satan thinks he is bothering you in an area, he will just keep pounding away. "You are going to die," he might say, or, "This is going to happen to you." If he sees that he has hit the mark, especially if you are suffering physically or have been diagnosed with a serious illness, the devil will just keep hammering away.

> **[The devil] was a murderer from the beginning and does not stand in the truth, because there is no truth in him. When he speaks a falsehood, he speaks what is natural to him, for he is a liar [himself] and the father of lies and of all that is false.**
>
> **John 8:44**

It is when we allow ourselves to meditate on, dwell on, and finally believe the devil's lies that fear gains a stronghold in our minds and hearts. That is why we should always meditate on God's Word, which brings faith and drives out all fear.

7

Walking Free from Guilt and Condemnation

Therefore, [there is] now no condemnation (no adjudging guilty of wrong) for those who are in Christ Jesus, who live [and] walk not after the dictates of the flesh, but after the dictates of the Spirit.

Romans 8:1

The devil will beat your brains out with guilt and condemnation if you allow him. Though it sounds too good to be true, God says, **I, even I, am He that blotteth out thy transgressions for mine own sake, and will not remember thy sins** (Isa. 43:25, KJV). As far as God is concerned, when you repent it is as if your sins never existed. He blots them out of His memory. You ought to blot them out of your memory too. It is Satan who is the accuser of the brethren (Rev. 12:10), and he will constantly bring up past mistakes and situations.

I am not giving you a license to sin, because I believe in living a holy life, but it would not be right if I did not tell you that God forgives and forgets about your sin when you repent and turn from it. You are "justified." That means "just as if it never happened." That is good news!

When I was in a church one time, the pastor's wife gave a powerful message in tongues. The young man who interpreted said, "Your mind is like a television set on a certain channel. Satan tries to come and change that to another station that promotes doubt, unbelief, and lack. Don't watch that channel. Turn it back to My channel, and view what I have said. Keep that before your eyes and in the midst of your heart." Keep your mind on the things of God.

Neurologists tell us that the brain controls the central nervous system. If you have an anxious thought, immediately the palpitation of your heart speeds up. You can feel your heart beating faster within your chest. Obviously, your mind affects your physical body.

God has put adrenalin, a hormone which increases endurance and muscular strength, inside every human being. All of us have heard of superhuman feats done in the face of adversity, such as lifting a car off a loved one or a friend. Impossible in the natural, but when adrenalin hits your blood stream, you are stronger than seven men for about seven minutes!

If guilt and condemnation are allowed to pound you continually, it is as though a bucket in your brain tips over, releasing adrenalin into your body. And if that is repeated frequently, your nervous system will get messed up. That is why it is so important to allow the Holy Spirit to search your heart every night before going to sleep.

If there is any guilt or condemnation, ask the Holy Spirit to tell you if there is something you need to repent of or if it is the devil trying to beat you down. If you need to repent, just repent and get cleansed according to 1 John 1:9. But if you haven't done anything wrong, rebuke that thing and get rid of it in Jesus' name!

It is time to walk free of guilt and condemnation and walk in the liberty in which Christ has set you free!

8

Putting Away Unforgiveness and Strife

Be gentle and forbearing with one another and, if one has a difference (a grievance or complaint) against another, readily pardoning each other; even as the Lord has [freely] forgiven you, so must you also [forgive].

And above all these [put on] love and enfold yourselves with the bond of perfectness [which binds everything together completely in ideal harmony].

Colossians 3:13,14

Unforgiveness and strife are big "welcome mats" to Satan, and they will open you up to all of his works. In this hour we need to close every door and remove every "welcome mat" that would give Satan license to steal, kill, and destroy in our lives.

In Matthew 18:21-35, Jesus gives good Holy Ghost Psychiatry guidelines on forgiveness.

Then Peter came up to Him and said, Lord, how many times may my brother sin against me and I forgive him and let it go? [As many as] up to seven times?

Jesus answered him, I tell you, not up to seven times, but seventy times seven!

Therefore the kingdom of heaven is like a human king who wished to settle accounts with his attendants.

When he began the accounting, one was brought to him who owed him ten thousand talents [probably about $10,000,000],

And because he could not pay, his master ordered him to be sold, with his wife and his children and everything that he possessed, and payment to be made.

So the attendant fell on his knees, begging him, Have patience with me and I will pay you everything.

And his master's heart was moved with compassion, and he released him and forgave him [cancelling] the debt.

But that same attendant, as he went out, found one of his fellow attendants who owed him a hundred denarii [about twenty dollars]; and he caught him by the throat and said, Pay what you owe!

So his fellow attendant fell down and begged him earnestly, Give me time, and I will pay you all!

But he was unwilling, and he went out and had him put in prison till he should pay the debt.

When his fellow attendants saw what had happened, they were greatly distressed, and they went and told everything that had taken place to their master.

Then his master called him and said to him, You contemptible and wicked attendant! I forgave and cancelled all that [great] debt of yours because you begged me to.

And should you not have had pity and mercy on your fellow attendant, as I had pity and mercy on you?

And in wrath his master turned him over to the torturers (the jailers), till he should pay all that he owed.

So also My heavenly Father will deal with every one of you, if you do not freely forgive your brother from your heart his offenses.

The New Testament states in several places that if you do not forgive, not only will you not be forgiven, but you will be delivered over to *tormentors*, which are evil spirits. In other words, there are things Christians can do which will throw the door open to Satan.

Second Timothy 2:24-26 gives Holy Ghost Psychiatry principles in the area of strife.

> **And the servant of the Lord must not be quarrelsome (fighting and contending). Instead, he must be kindly to everyone and mild-tempered [preserving the bond of peace]; he must be a skilled and suitable teacher, patient and forbearing and willing to suffer wrong.**
>
> **He must correct his opponents with courtesy and gentleness, in the hope that God may grant that they will repent and come to know the Truth [that they will perceive and recognize and become accurately acquainted with and acknowledge it],**
>
> **And that they may come to their senses [and] escape out of the snare of the devil, having been held captive by him, [henceforth] to do His [God's] will.**

I once heard another minister, teaching on excellence in ministry, share about dealing with employees in the area of strife. He said, "I'll go a long way with my employees in any area of struggle or battle except in the area of strife. When they get into strife, they are gone in a New York second!"

Why is his ministry so adamant about no strife? Because where strife exists, there is confusion and every evil work. It must be dealt with. James 3:14-16 (KJV) says,

> **But if ye have bitter envying and strife in your hearts, glory not, and lie not against the truth. This wisdom descendeth not from above, but is earthly, sensual, devilish. For where envying and strife is, there is confusion and every evil work.**

The Amplified Bible says,

> **But if you have bitter jealousy (envy) and contention (rivalry, selfish ambition) in your hearts, do not pride yourselves on it and thus be in defiance of and false to the Truth.**

> **This [superficial] wisdom is not such as comes
> down from above, but is earthly, unspiritual (animal),
> even devilish (demoniacal).**
>
> **For wherever there is jealousy (envy) and
> contention (rivalry and selfish ambition), there will
> also be confusion (unrest, disharmony, rebellion) and
> all sorts of evil and vile practices.**

One of the television stations we were on offered to air
our program at a very low rate if Sharon and I would do a
live telethon for them twice a year. We consented to do it.

After we had flown to the city where the station was
located and done the telethon, the owner of the station took
us to his home. He was born again, filled with the Spirit of
God, and appeared to love God with all of his heart, but I
believe he was a deceived man. He started saying some
nasty, derogatory things about a minister I listen to on a
consistent basis, someone who has been a help and blessing
to me and to thousands of others.

I did not want to be rude, and I certainly did not want to
be thrown off his television station, but I politely had to tell
this man that I did not want to hear accusations like that.
He continued, so I calmly repeated my request that we not
discuss this minister in that negative manner. When he still
kept on, I had to ask him to take us back to the hotel. It was
"cold city" the rest of that time.

If I had let the devil plant this kind of seed through that
man, it would have given the devil something to play with
in my life, as well as in his life. I refuse to hear anything
negative about other ministries. I refuse to receive an
accusation against an elder. I am talking about how to have
a sound, peaceful mind. Ephesians 4:31 (KJV) says,

> **Let all bitterness, and wrath, and anger, and
> clamour, and evil speaking, be put away from you, with
> all malice.**

Fretting and clamoring are close cousins to strife. I
remember one Sunday morning after church, my wife and I

were carrying several things into the house. As I went to unlock the door, the baby started crying. I reached for the key and got the wrong one. On top of that, it was cold outside and Sharon made a comment for me to hurry up, which I thought was critical. It was chaos! However, I realized we were beginning to get into strife and said, "Let's stop this. The devil is trying to get us to have a rotten afternoon."

Proverbs 17:14 says, **The beginning of strife is as when water first trickles [from a crack in a dam]; therefore stop contention before it becomes worse and quarreling breaks out.** If you are not careful, fretting and clamoring will turn into strife. Why are you told to put these things away? Does God want to put a star by your name in heaven and call you Dudley Doright? No! He knows that these things open your life to the devil. He does not want the devil to have an opening to get to you.

Guard Your Words

Sharon and I have been in settings where we were talking and enjoying ourselves with other ministers when suddenly, on the inside of me, there was an uneasiness about something I had said. It is hard to define spiritual things with natural words, but Ephesians 4:30 (KJV) says, **Grieve not the holy Spirit of God.** There will be a grief or a check in my spirit, and the umpire of my life, the Holy Spirit will say, "You've said enough." Proverbs 10:19 says,

> **In a multitude of words transgression is not lacking, but** *he who restrains his lips is prudent.*

Ephesians 4:29,30 says,

> **Let no foul or polluting language, nor evil word, nor unwholesome or worthless talk [ever] come out of your mouth; but only such [speech] as is good and beneficial to the spiritual progress of others, as is fitting to the need and the occasion, that it may be a**

blessing and give grace (God's favor) to those who hear it.

And do not grieve the Holy Spirit of God (do not offend or vex or sadden Him), by Whom you were sealed (marked, branded as God's own, secured) for the day of redemption — of final deliverance through Christ from evil and the consequences of sin.

Pray Psalm 141:3 over yourself right now:

Set a guard, O Lord, before my mouth; keep watch at the door of my lips.

These verses are keys to peace of mind and to keeping yourself off limits to the devil where unforgiveness and strife are concerned. He cannot build any strongholds of bitterness or wrath in your mind if you meditate and practice these scriptures.

9

Allowing God's Peace
to Be Your Umpire

And let the peace (soul harmony which comes)
from the Christ rule (act as umpire continually) in your
hearts — deciding and settling with finality all
questions that arise in your minds — [in that peaceful
state] to which as [members of Christ's] one body you
were also called [to live]. And be thankful —
appreciative, giving praise to God always.

Colossians 3:15

Knowledge of sports is not really my strength, but I
know enough to know that an umpire acts with finality on
every play. If a guy slides into home base and the umpire
calls him safe, he is safe. If the umpire calls him out, no
matter what it looks like, he is out. The spectators may
curse or jeer and throw beer bottles at the umpire, but if he
calls someone out, that is it.

Certainly umpires are capable of making mistakes at
times. But the umpire on the inside of you, the Holy Spirit,
never makes mistakes. Allow Him to answer with finality
every question that arises in your mind, knowing that His
calls always bring total peace to your inner man. Let the
peace of God act as your umpire.

I act as umpire sometimes — acting and deciding with
finality — when it comes to things my little son, Anthony,
does. When he was two years old, he loved to play in the
toilet bowl. He loved to take his little hands and make the
water go swish, swish, swish! There were all kinds of germs

57

in the toilet bowl, but he did not know it. I did not mind him playing with water, but not toilet water!

He did a lot of adventuresome things like that. He would pry open the door to the basement and stand at the top of the basement steps. I would holler, "No, no, get back here!" In the same way, we may not know why, but there are all kinds of things to which God says, "No, no, get back here! That isn't good."

"God, what am I going to do about this? What am I going to do about my husband (or wife)?" We are not smart enough to figure out all the answers, but we have God's help, and sometimes He says, "No."

The devil will try to meddle with your mind, tempting you with wrong thoughts and confusing you about a situation. Whenever you feel confusion and distress, not knowing which way to turn, turn to the Holy Spirit. Let Him answer with finality every question that arises in your heart and mind.

When you get a check in your spirit or a "no" from the Holy Spirit, listen and act accordingly. He knows what is ahead. Someone may be planning to give you something you are considering buying or perhaps the price is going to drop significantly very soon. It bothers me when I buy something without consulting the Holy Spirit, and the next day in the paper the same item is advertised for half price. It bothers Sharon even more, and she usually takes it back!

How can you know the will of God? One way to know His will is whether you have peace deep on the inside of you. Any time there is a violation or an interruption of peace on the inside of you, something is wrong.

There have been many times when I have said, "Sharon, something is bothering me. I don't quite know what it is." Then I will stay before God, looking for the answer. Maybe that same day or two days later, it will come up in me and the Spirit of God will tell me what I should do. Sometimes there are things I have to correct. Sometimes I have to judge a situation. Sometimes the timing is not right.

When I seek the Lord, I say, "By faith I receive the answer. You are going to speak to me, or I am just going to end up knowing the answer in my heart." If I lack peace, sometimes I will ask Sharon what is in her heart. If she answers, "I don't know," I will ask, "Do you have peace in your heart?" If she responds, "It seems like there is an unrest," then I make a decision to hold back. Do not violate your own heart.

The inner witness of peace from the Holy Spirit, or what I sometimes call soul peace, is a barometer for determining the will of God. There will always be a witness in your heart. Follow your heart rather than what someone says.

Remember, all kinds of thoughts may come to your head. The devil is the imitator. He emulates God. The Word of God will help you to discern between what is of God and what is of the devil, because the Word always lines up with God's will. They are one and the same. And just like the Holy Spirit, the Word will give you peace.

Did the thought come from the outside, or did it come from your spirit up to your brain? *God will speak from the inside out, and the devil will always speak from the outside in.* Ultimately, what the devil says will cause unrest, but what the Holy Spirit says will give you a peace that passes all understanding. Then you can act in confidence, knowing you are in God's will.

10
Casting Your Cares Upon the Lord

Therefore humble yourselves (demote, lower yourselves in your own estimation) under the mighty hand of God, that in due time He may exalt you.

Casting the whole of your care — all your anxieties, all your worries, all your concerns, once and for all — on Him; for He cares for you affectionately and cares about you watchfully.

First Peter 5:6,7

One time when I was meditating on verse seven, the Lord spoke to me, "Put your fear *far from you.*" In other words, cast all your cares, anxieties, worries, and concerns far from you.

Most anxious thoughts are about things that are in the future. There was an old song back in the sixties that said, "Like a rubber ball, I keep bouncing back to you." Concerns, anxieties, worries, and cares are like rubber balls that keep bouncing back at you. You can pick them back up and keep playing with them, but the Bible says to cast them *once and for all* upon the Lord.

As I have said before, in the past a flurry of things would come to my mind every night at bedtime: decisions I had to make, what I had to do at some future time, how I was going to pay certain bills. (Sometimes I had to have $12,000 a month just for property payments, not counting all of the other thousands of dollars each month for other additional expenses.) Those thoughts would come to me at night, and instead of getting the rest I needed I would toss and turn, worrying about those things.

At times I would wake up in the middle of the night and my mind would start whirling. I would stay awake fretting about various situations for hours. After a period of time, this anxiety and sleeplessness took its toll on my physical body.

Thank God, I have learned how to deal with Satan's attempts at harassing me. I no longer give place to thoughts of business at bedtime or in the middle of the night. Now I say, "No, devil. I don't care. It's not time to think about that. It's time to sleep." I have learned to cast all my cares upon the Lord, knowing whatever I face tomorrow, He has already provided the answer. Remember:

WORRY IS LIKE PAYING INTEREST ON A LOAN YOU MAY NEVER HAVE TO BORROW.

I remember when I was a policemen working on the midnight shift. One morning about two thirty we received a call to assist some other policemen trying to break up a bar fight. When we arrived, I saw a guy who looked like a wrestler beating up the cops and scattering them all over the place. It reminded me of how Jesus must have handled the devil and all the demons in hell.

Jesus defeated all demonic principalities and whipped the devil in the pit of hell. Then He walked over to the devil's keyboard and took the keys of death, hell, and the grave. He walked out, unlocked paradise, and led the captives into liberty! Isn't that wonderful?

Then Jesus said, **All authority — all power of rule — in heaven and on earth has been given to Me** (Matt. 28:18). This is the same power that Jesus confers upon men, women, boys, and girls when they receive Him as Lord and Savior. We are *equipped* with that same power. If the devil himself and every demon in the world came to your house, the name of Jesus would be enough to throw them all out in the street on their ear! That is good news!

When the devil comes at you with worry thoughts and anxiety ideas, you may need to declare every five minutes, "I have cast all my cares, anxieties, worries, and concerns on the Lord. I will not take them back because He has them." You should do this especially before you go to sleep and let your last thoughts be of the goodness of God.

In dealing with the death of my parents, there were tremendous cares to be cast on the Lord. When a born-again friend or loved one goes on to be with the Lord, you will naturally grieve. But if the grief does not subside with time and your heart begin to heal, it is not a natural grieving any longer. Now the grief is coming from the devil, and it's time to take authority over it in Jesus' name and begin to fix your mind on God. Isaiah 26:3 says,

> **You will guard him and keep him in perfect and constant peace whose mind [both its inclination and its character] is stayed on You, because he commits himself to You, leans on You and hopes confidently in You.**

How do you fix your mind on God? By meditating day and night in His Word. Even if you are at the lowest state possible, if you will do what the Word says, your heart will start mending and your life will begin to return to normal.

I heard a Christian brother say one time, "I put on my spiritual clothes every day." Now, when my eyes blink open in the morning, I start clothing myself. I put the blood of Jesus Christ over my mind and over my heart. I put on the helmet of salvation and the breastplate of righteousness, for I am the very righteousness of God in Christ Jesus.

I take the shield of faith so I can quench every fiery dart of the enemy. Not only do I have defensive weaponry, but I have offensive weaponry. I will take the sword of the Spirit, which is the Word of God, and come against every nasty devil. Those demons got a poor assignment when they were assigned to me, because I will hurt them with the Word.

My feet are shod with the preparation of the gospel of peace. My loins are gird about with truth, because my wife and I walk in moral excellence and integrity. Because I live a fasted, temperate life, I have put on my rear guard also. In the Greek language, one of the meanings of the word "fasting" means "to put your rear guard on."

In order to cast the whole of your care upon the Lord, there are certain things you must reject, like thoughts of fear, worry, doubt, and unbelief. Assume for a moment that a package is delivered to your house. The delivery man says to you, "I have a package for you. Just sign right here."

Before you take it you ask him, "What's in it?"

"Rattlesnakes," he answers.

"No, I don't want it." (You do not have to sign for that package!)

"Well, it's yours," he responds. "Someone sent it to you."

"I don't care. I'm not signing for it. I'm not going to take possession of rattlesnakes just because someone sent them to me!"

You do not have to receive the cares and concerns and worries — the rattlesnakes — that the devil wants to "give" you, either!

11
Don't Cast Away Your Confidence

Do not, therefore, fling away your fearless confidence, for it carries a great and glorious compensation of reward.

For you have need of steadfast patience and endurance, so that you may perform and fully accomplish the will of God, and thus receive and carry away [and enjoy to the full] what is promised.

Hebrews 10:35,36

For years I have been training myself to respond to any challenge by asking, "What does the Word say?" Something pops up and I ask, "What does the Word say about that?" I call this "thinking in chapter and verse." I am trying to get to the point where I do this automatically. The fight of faith takes place in your mind, and thinking in chapter and verse is *how* you fight. It is thinking in chapter and verse that gives you confidence and keeps you confident.

Be well balanced — temperate, sober of mind; be vigilant and cautious at all times, for that enemy of yours, the devil, roams around like a lion roaring [in fierce hunger], seeking someone to seize upon and devour.

Withstand him; be firm in faith [against his onset], — rooted, established, strong, immovable, and determined — knowing that the same (identical) sufferings are appointed to your brotherhood (the whole body of Christians) throughout the world.

First Peter 5:8,9

I can hear someone say, "But Brother Crank, the doctor told me this." He probably was right, but that is the *natural* report. Now ask yourself, *"What does the Word say?"* If you are thinking in chapter and verse, you will stand firm in faith, knowing that by the stripes of Jesus you *were* healed. (1 Pet. 2:24.)

If you will stand firm in faith and not waver, you will receive from the Lord. You may be thinking, "I might waver and I'll die." If you waver, you will know it because you will lose hope and your faith will become weak. As soon as you recognize that this has happened, just repent and get back in the Word. If you will stay in the Word, God will keep you until His promise of healing comes to pass in your life.

Not only does the Word of God give you confidence, but so does the Holy Spirit. There are seven attributes or characteristics we can see in the Holy Spirit. He is your Comforter, Counselor, Helper, Advocate, Intercessor, Strengthener, and Standby. (John 15:26.)

As your Standby, the Holy Spirit will back you up through every situation. He will tell you exactly what to do and then give you the courage and strength to do it as you step out in faith. No matter what your doctor, your lawyer, or anyone else says, *you* ask the Holy Spirit, "What should I do?" Then do it with total confidence. You will make it regardless of what you are facing, for First Corinthians 10:13 (KJV) says,

> **There hath no temptation taken you but such as is common to man: but God is faithful, Who will not suffer you to be tempted above that ye are able; but will with the temptation also make a way to escape, that ye may be able to bear it.**

When you go through something, the devil will tell you that you are the only person who has ever gone through it and that you are too weak or unequipped to make it. He is a liar, because many people have gone through the exact same thing, and God says in His Word that you will never go through anything you cannot overcome. I realize you have probably seen some make it and others not make it. But you will make it, because you are going to withstand Satan as you stand firm in the faith, resisting the temptation to be a worrier!

I come from a family of champion worriers. My dad was one of the greatest worriers in the world. The only thing that defeated him was what was in his mind. He worried about everything. When I was about twelve years old, he thought he was going to die of a heart attack. Somebody told him to drink raw eggs, so every day he drank raw eggs. But he continued to believe that he was going to die from a heart attack. Eventually he did die prematurely.

Where is the balance? Go to the doctor once a year and have a physical, but do not dwell on bad reports or frightening things you pick up from a television program or magazine. Do not let those negative things dwell on the inside of you. Keep the Word in the midst of your heart, for the Word is life and health to all your flesh.

No matter what circumstances you are facing, do not cast away your confidence! Galatians 6:9 says, **And let us not lose heart *and* grow weary *and* faint in acting nobly *and* doing right, for in due time *and* at the appointed season we shall reap, if we do not loosen *and* relax our courage *and* faint.**

If we think in chapter and verse, draw on the strength of the Holy Spirit, and don't faint, we will come out the winner every time!

12

Satan's Greatest Delight: Choking Out the Word

I have heard Dr. Billy Graham say numerous times, "You can't keep birds from flying over your head, but you can keep them from building a nest in your hair." Satan will constantly bombard your mind with negative thoughts, because he knows if he can get to you in your mind, he can affect your entire life.

Proverbs 16:28 says, **A whisperer separates close friends.** Satan is a whisperer, and he will whisper things to you to negate the truth of God's Word and separate you from your Best Friend, Jesus. This is why you must be vigilant in protecting your mind with God's Word. Jesus said in Mark 4:18,19 (KJV):

> **And these are they which are sown among thorns; such as hear the word, And the cares of this world, and the deceitfulness of riches, and the lusts of other things entering in, choke the word, and it becometh unfruitful.**

Satan wants to choke out the Word of God on the inside of you, because that is what gives you sanity and soundness of mind. Personally, if it were not for the Bible, I probably would have gone crazy from the panic attacks, but the Word is what kept me on the right track and eventually brought total healing.

As I read the Word, the Spirit of God may correct me. Sometimes I have to repent and make some adjustments, either in my thinking or in something I am doing. Jesus is the best psychiatrist in the world. He made the human brain and the mind, and He knows all about us.

All sin, and the chaos, clamor, murders, rapes, robberies, and abortions that it consists of, came as a result of Adam and Eve not listening to the Word of God. Satan came to Eve and asked a question that she rolled around in her mind: **Hath God said?** (Gen. 3:1 KJV). In the end, Adam let Satan's question, rather than God's Word, dominate his mind also. This thought, which questioned what God had said, was the entrance through which spiritual death came to the entire human race.

Years ago I heard John Osteen share about the compassion of God that came on him to pray for his sister who was in ill health. He had not seen her for years. He said, "As I was praying one day, the Spirit of the Lord rose up on the inside of me, and I started praying for my sister. The Bible says that the love of God is shed abroad in our hearts by the Holy Ghost, and suddenly the love of God just started pouring out of me for my sister."

John drove to the city in Texas where his sister lived and went with the local pastor to his sister's home. She had not been out of bed for months, and a nurse was caring for her. John said, "She looked wild and was at death's door. When I looked at her, a holy anger rose up in me. I said, 'I don't care what the devil said. You are not suffering this for the glory of God!'

"I jumped right in the middle of the bed and said, 'Come out of her, devil.' The power of God hit that place. She jumped out of the bed and started shouting. Then she washed up, combed her hair, and was in her right mind again."

You can find unbelief in many denominations. John's sister had been in a church that taught that physical sickness and mental illness were crosses to bear. A voice had spoken to her and said, "I want to put a cross of mental illness on you so that you will have compassion to pray for those who are mentally ill."

The Apostle Paul said, **But though we, or an angel from heaven, preach any other gospel unto you than that which we have preached unto you, let him be accursed** (Gal. 1:8 KJV). The Scripture will settle the source of every thought that arises in your mind. Anything the Holy Spirit speaks will *always* line up with God's Word. In this case, the Bible clearly says that by His stripes you *were* healed. (1 Pet. 2:24.)

Maybe the devil has not been able to get you to indulge in adultery, fornication, or what some call "big sins." But he has told you, "You are going to have to suffer with this sickness for two years because of what you did." That is not from God! God tells us that today is the day of salvation. You can be forgiven and healed *today*. One of the greatest keys to having and maintaining soundness of mind is acquiring sound doctrine. Check everything you are hearing with the Word of God.

The Holy Spirit will also help you to stay on track. I have had homosexuals come into my services and I cast the devil out of them. Later some of them have told me, "When I came into the service, something told me that I hated you. I couldn't stand you." What was it that caused them to hate me instantly? It was the spirit that was *on* them hating the Spirit that is *in* me!

The Holy Spirit will decide with finality every question that arises. Satan will try to build sand castles in your head: "Your husband doesn't love you anymore. He doesn't care for you." Or, "Your wife is cheating on you." He will try to bombard you with fearful, anxious, despondent thoughts. But the Comforter will help you bring your thoughts back in line with God's Word.

The devil used to try to fight me with claustrophobia, the fear of being enclosed. We were traveling in ministry and living in a little trailer which we parked next to a different church about every week. We had everything we owned in that little trailer, plus crying babies and no money to do anything. I dreaded the winter months, knowing that I had to spend them cooped up in that little cubicle. But fear is an evil spirit, and it can be resisted. To overcome claustrophobia, I began to say, "I resist you in Jesus' name."

Years ago, I also had a fear of crossing huge bridges. One time we had to cross a big bridge over the Mississippi River from Cape Girardeau, Missouri, to Mounds City, Illinois. In the middle of the bridge my son, David, just a little boy at the time, said, "Daddy, what if this bridge falls down right now?"

All of a sudden, fear came on me. I had not really been thinking about it until he said something. To overcome this fear, I did the same thing I did to overcome claustrophobia. I refused to entertain thoughts and pictures in my mind about bridges collapsing and meditated on the Word of God instead, seeing those mighty protecting angels surrounding us.

We need to guard *every thought* and check it out to see whether or not it is in line with Scripture. This is why we must put the Word of God in our hearts and meditate on it every day.

Sharon and I are watchful about what we hear, even on Christian radio and TV programs. One of us will come into the room when the other is watching TV and say, "You'd better turn that one off." Sharon will do that even when I am listening to a preacher if he is preaching doubt and unbelief! But as soon as she gives me that wake-up call, I will say, "I am headed for the clicker" and immediately turn it off.

I do not want that stuff in my spirit, because God said, **Keep your heart with all vigilance and above all that you**

guard, for out of it flow the springs of life (Prov. 4:23). *The King James Version* says, **Keep thy heart with all diligence; for out of it are the issues of life.**

I do not listen to the news very much any more (maybe five percent of it) because the Bible says the cares of this world will choke the Word on the inside of you. If you listen to the negative news long enough, fear will get a hold on you.

What should you do when fear of sickness and disease comes on you, or when something happens to your sister, your daddy, or your mama? Immediately, Satan will take an event and try to build it up on the inside of you, even if it takes him ten years.

To combat these thoughts, *You need to think the thoughts of God.* "Jesus was wounded for my transgressions and bruised for my iniquities. The chastisement of my peace was upon Him, and with His stripes I am healed." (See Is. 53:5.)

One time when I was with my brother, he said, "That's strange."

I asked, "What?"

He said, "Our sister wears glasses, Mama wore glasses, Daddy wore glasses, and I wear bifocals. How come you are the only one in the family who doesn't wear glasses? Is your vision still 20/20?"

I said, "It's still 20/20."

A long time ago, when my eyes were very good, I started confessing healing. I have always confessed that I have excellent sight and hearing. As a result, I have not needed glasses. Even if you wear glasses now, *confess what God's Word says about you.*

Jesus says your healing was paid for in full at Calvary, regardless of the symptoms that may be evident in your body today. Do not let Satan bombard you with his thoughts, but start building faith on the inside of you by believing and speaking what God's Word says about you.

We must always keep the Word before our eyes to be free of worries, anxieties, cares, and concerns. Soundness of mind comes from thinking God's thoughts.

When Anthony was very young, he would bring me sodas until I had six or seven in my lap. That game gets old after awhile, and sometimes I was just not in the mood for it. Then he would pick up something else and start bringing it to me until I finally said, "Stop!" Until I convinced him I did not want it and I was not going to take it, he kept bringing things to me.

Although the devil's motive is totally ugly compared to the love and innocence of a child, he is persistent like that. Until you convince him you are not taking his deliveries, he will keep coming. Even at the point where you say, "I can't take it, I can't take but one more day of this," the devil will say, "Oh, good! We've got permission to keep harassing you for at least one more day!" He is not going to trot on down the block until he knows you mean business.

Satan, the one who imitates a rip-roaring lion, wants to destroy your peace of mind with worries, cares, concerns, and anxieties. Do not let him choke the Word out of your life and resist him with the Word, because believing and trusting the Word makes your life free from worry and full of peace.

13
Prayer Will Strengthen Your Inner Man

Prayer is so important in dealing with the mind. In the Garden of Gethsemane before His crucifixion, Jesus gathered around Him those closest to Him to pray because of the severity of the trial He was facing.

Then Jesus went with them to a place called Gethsemane, and He told His disciples, Sit down here while I go over yonder and pray.

And taking with Him Peter and the two sons of Zebedee, *He began to show grief and distress of mind and was deeply depressed.*

Then He said to them, My soul is very sad and deeply grieved, so that I am almost dying of sorrow. Stay here and keep awake and keep watch with Me.

And going a little farther, He threw Himself upon the ground on His face and prayed saying, My Father, if it is possible, let this cup pass away from Me; nevertheless, not what I will — not what I desire — but as You will and desire.

And He came to the disciples and found them sleeping, and He said to Peter, What! Are you so utterly unable to stay awake and keep watch with Me for one hour?

All of you must keep awake (give strict attention, be cautious and active) and watch and pray, that you may not come into temptation. The spirit indeed is willing, but the flesh is weak.

Again a second time He went away and prayed, My Father, if this cannot pass by unless I drink it, Your will be done.

And again He came and found them sleeping, for their eyes were weighed down with sleep.

So, leaving them again, He went away and prayed for the third time, using the same words.

Then He returned to the disciples and said to them, Are you still sleeping and taking your rest? Behold, the hour is at hand, and the Son of Man is betrayed into the hands of especially wicked sinners —whose way or nature it is to act in opposition to God.

Get up, let us be going! See, My betrayer is at hand!

Matthew 26:36-46

The reason Jesus was able to stand the psychological pressure of facing the reality of being separated from the Father during the crucifixion was because prayer strengthened His inner man.

Every day I pray, "Holy Ghost, strengthen my inner man by Your presence." Then I pray in tongues, building myself up on my most holy faith (Jude 20) to the point where I can make my mind kick out the circumstances I am facing. Instead, I begin to think "in chapter and verse."

Real prayer and what some people call prayer are two different things. We are not to go to God and pray the problem. Real prayer is going to God with His Word, which contains the answer. An example of this is praying Second Corinthians 2:14: "Thank you, Father, that in Christ You always lead me to triumph as a trophy of Christ's victory. I am facing such-and-such a situation (it is okay to tell Him), and I thank You in advance for causing me to triumph in this thing."

As you pray the Word and think in chapter and verse, you will begin to think the thoughts of God, rejecting the fearful, anxious thoughts from Satan. Your faith will grow, your mind will be sound, and you will have confidence. That is good Holy Ghost Psychiatry!

One time I asked a lady in my congregation to pray about something that was coming against me. She gave me a tape in which the speaker said, "I feel like the Lord is telling me to tell you, 'This too shall pass.'" God had also used a song to illuminate this same message to me, "This too shall pass."

As you look back at problems and trials you faced five years ago, you realize, "That wasn't nearly as big as I thought it was." Remembering the victories God has brought you in the past helps you put what you are going through now in perspective. Even though the present problem may seem horrendously big, God helped you out of your problems before, and what you are facing now too shall pass.

Make a daily appointment with God for a time of prayer. Pour out your heart, declare the Word over your situation, pray in tongues when you don't know what to pray (Rom. 8:26) and ask the Holy Spirit to speak to you. Praise and thank Him for all He has done, is doing, and will do in your behalf. And most important, listen to Him. Prayer is your special time with God to grow more intimate with Him. Only prayer like this can give you a proper perspective and an inner strength to walk through each day's challenges with victory!

14
Rejoice Regardless
of Your Circumstances

Mental illness is at an all-time high right now, but I believe it will be at an all-time low in the ranks of God's children *if we look to His Word and believe what God says will triumph rather than the circumstances.*

The devil wants to drive you crazy, but Paul gives some advice by the inspiration of the Holy Spirit that will keep you rejoicing regardless of circumstances. He says in Colossians 3:16:

> **Let the word [spoken by] the Christ, the Messiah, have its home (in your hearts and minds) and dwell in you in [all its] richness, as you teach and admonish and train one another in all insight and intelligence and wisdom [in spiritual things, and sing] psalms and hymns and spiritual songs, making melody to God with [His] grace in your hearts.**

It is good spiritual psychiatry to your mind to sing psalms, hymns, and spiritual songs. Practicing this will help you to be more alert to the Holy Spirit and what He is speaking in your spirit. Paul said, **Rejoice in the Lord always — delight, gladden yourselves in Him; again I say, Rejoice!** (Phil. 4:4).

Sharon is always humming spiritual songs. That is how she keeps her spirit active, energized, and strengthened. In Psalm 112:7, the psalmist David said, **He (the righteous) shall not be afraid of *evil tidings*: his heart is firmly fixed, trusting (leaning on and being confident) in the Lord.**

Now if anyone had a lot of bad news during his life, it was David. But he learned that bad news may be initially unsettling, but it does not need to shake us. We can gladden ourselves in the Lord. Our confident trust and hope are to be in Him — not in the predictions, situations, and circumstances of the world. This is good Holy Ghost Psychiatry!

The Bible says that God literally inhabits or dwells in the praises of His people. That means that when we praise and worship Him, sing psalms and hymns and spiritual songs, and make melody in our hearts — which is rejoicing — then He shows up. He is on the scene to give us whatever we need.

If you rejoice always, no matter what is happening to you or around you, you will have the mind of Christ and a heart that rests in the Lord. In that condition, it is impossible for the devil to get any thoughts of fear, anxiety, or panic rooted in your mind or heart!

15
God Is For You!

Do not fret or have any anxiety about anything, but in every circumstance and in everything, by prayer and petition [definite requests], with thanksgiving, continue to make your wants known to God.

And God's peace [be yours, that tranquil state of a soul assured of its salvation through Christ, and *so fearing nothing from God* and being content with its earthly lot of whatever sort that is, that peace] which transcends all understanding shall garrison and mount guard over your hearts and minds in Christ Jesus.

Philippians 4:6,7

Fearing nothing from God . . . . One of the most common threats the devil uses is: GOD IS GOING TO GET YOU! If God was going to get us for our sin, we would have already been had! I want to tell you something. God is on your side! He is for you! He is on your team!

All of my kids are fabulous, and if they get hurt or run into trouble of some kind, I will try to get them out of it no matter what it takes — mentally, physically, financially. I will endeavor to get them out of it if it can be done, and I am just an earthly father. There is no way I love my kids as much as our Heavenly Father loves us, and there is no way I love my kids as much as God loves me.

In John 17:23, Jesus said something that is hard for the brain to comprehend. It is mind-boggling!

I in them, and You in Me, in order that they may become one and perfectly united, that the world may know and [definitely] recognize that You sent Me, and that *You have loved them [even] as you have loved Me.*

81

God is on your side. The devil always tries to paint God as some austere figure or some old man Who is behind the times, holding a whip, and waiting for you to do something wrong so He can hit you on the head. That is not God! The Bible says He draws us with His love. He is kind and tender. He will judge the world, but He loves you.

Years ago, as I was praying in preparation for a meeting, the anointing of God came on me and I started praying strongly in the Spirit. Then I began to prophesy. I will not share all of the things I prophesied, but God said some things concerning the future. He said, "Satan will always try to make molehills look like mountains." And He told me to quit overreacting to some things that were going on in my life.

I knew it was a word from God, because I did have a tendency to overreact sometimes. That Word has really helped me. Satan is always trying to be in control in a situation, and he gains control in the mind when you receive thoughts that blow things way out of proportion. He will tell you all kinds of things:

"Something awful is going to happen to you."

"You are getting old, and you can't do this anymore."

These thoughts are simply trying to make the problem bigger than God. Then the next step is to think that God doesn't care or He wouldn't have let this happen to you. And yet, I have learned that when problems come up — and believe me they will — God always has someone or something around the corner ready to provide a way out, even if it is at the last second! God has always helped me through, and He will always help you too.

To know that *God is for you* is one of the principles of Holy Ghost Psychiatry that will serve you for the rest of your life. It dictates the end result of *every* skirmish you will ever have with the devil. Why? Because knowing God loves you and is for you gives you the faith and confidence to stand on His Word and not faint! In Christ, there is no defeat!

16
Learning To Be Content

And God's peace [be yours, that tranquil state of a
soul assured of its salvation through Christ, and so
fearing nothing from God and *content with its earthly
lot of whatever sort that is.*

Philippians 4:7

Being content with your earthly lot does not mean God
will leave you in the state you are in right now. Still, He
wants you to learn to be content regardless of the
circumstances.

There are people who are worth two million dollars and
they are not content. They are now pushing for the four
million dollar mark, and when they get there they will set a
new goal of six million dollars. They are never content. You
need to be content right where you are, because if you are
not content, it will mess you up psychologically.

It is the devil who tries to get you to be discontented. He
tries to get marriage partners discontented with each other
by introducing such thoughts as, "Look at that guy with the
young wife. You've been married for forty years, man. You
need to trade her in for two twenties." Resist his divisive
thoughts with God's thoughts.

For the rest, brethren, whatever is true, whatever is
worthy of reverence and is honorable and seemly,
whatever is just, whatever is pure, whatever is lovely
and lovable, whatever is kind and winsome and
gracious, if there is any virtue and excellence, if there is
anything worthy of praise, think on and weigh and take
account of these things — fix your minds on them.

> **Practice what you have learned and received and heard and seen in me, and model your way of living on it, and the God of peace — of untroubled, undisturbed well-being — will be with you.**
>
>

Philippians 4:8,9

There is not a person living who is not looking for **untroubled, undisturbed well-being!** But listen to what Paul writes in Philippians 4:11:

> **Not that I am implying that I was in any personal want, for I have learned how to be content (satisfied to the point where I am not disturbed or disquieted) in whatever state I am.**

Paul had to *learn* to be content, and so do you and I. For those of us who have suffered a panic attack, learning to be content in all situations and circumstances is a top priority! We learn to be content by meditating in God's Word and letting the Holy Spirit comfort us and teach us in every situation. We have to accept the fact that the devil is going to try to upset us and drive us over the edge, but at the same time stand confidently that God is greater than anything the devil can throw at us!

Learning to be content means we learn to deal with the realities of life according to God's Word and not our emotions. We know that everything is subject to change except God's Word. When the fight is over, God's Word will be the one left standing every time — and that brings contentment!

17
There Is Always Hope!

As I wrote this material on panic attacks I came under the greatest attack on my life and ministry since the late eighties. I choose to call this "ironic and demonic!" However, it has honestly amazed me that through this bizarre and traumatic time for my family and my ministry, I felt the fearful anticipations and beginnings of a panic attack from time to time and still never actually had one. This is almost unbelievable in my own comprehension, and it is a commendation to Almighty God that His Word is true.

I love this happy thought of John Osteen's, "And it came to pass." Whatever you're going through, it came but it will pass! You are going to come out of this and be better and stronger than ever. What Satan meant for evil in your life, and even all the mistakes and sins you have committed against your own body, God will turn to your good. (See Romans 8:28.)

One day, you're going to be right where I am right now, looking back at this with a smile on your face saying, "Lord, truly your Word is so. You have restored my soul. And now I'm using what the devil tried to destroy me to help other people."

When David was at Ziklag (2 Samuel, chapter 30) it was one of the worst times he had ever experienced. Saul had had contracts out on his life for years, and when he got back home to Ziklag the enemy had stolen his wives and everything he owned. The situation was so bad, even his friends spoke of stoning him. Talk about potential for a panic attack!

But do you know what David did? The Bible says, "And David encouraged himself." After he began encouraging himself, David said, "Shall I pursue?" And the Lord said, "Pursue and you'll recover it all." And that's my word to you on how to get over a panic attack — encourage yourself. Once you encourage yourself then God can move miraculously to deliver you and set you on your course toward fulfilling His call on your life.

Most theologians agree that *within 72 hours of the worst time David ever went through in his life, he was sitting on the throne of Israel!* I want you to know, even though dealing with fear, anxiety, and panic attacks is a terrible ordeal, something good and wonderful is going to come out of this — and that is a great hope!

Romans 15:13 calls God **the God of hope**. The Greek word for hope is not, "I wish it was," but "confident expectation, a happy anticipation of a coming good." **Now faith is the substance of things hoped for** (happily anticipated), **the evidence of things not seen**. You're going to come through this! I came through this and you will too.

My recovery didn't happen overnight. It was gradual. It actually took several years for me to come out of this, but I sit here today telling you that Psalm 23 is true. He restored my soul and led me to the still waters. He got me out of hot water! He got me out of problem waters! He got me out of white water! He got me out of storms in water! And He led me to still, calm waters and restored my soul.

Today, if any pressure, anxiety, or thoughts of worry and fear assault my mind, dozens of scriptures flood my soul. I have made a list of these key scriptures in the last chapter of this book. Read them, study them, memorize them, and meditate on them until they are a part of you.

They will give you supernatural strength, soundness of mind, and peace.

Today I don't need natural medication to get to the spiritual medication! I go straight to the Word of God on the inside of me for whatever I need. **Now thanks be to God which always causes me to triumph in Christ** (2 Cor. 2:14). The hope I set before you is that you can one day know the same freedom from fear, anxiety, and panic attacks!

18

Word Prescriptions
for Soundness of Mind

If you will meditate and "chew on" the select scriptures which follow, your soundness of mind will be greatly enhanced. However, do *not* limit your meditation of the Word to these few selections. Get into all of the Bible, and you will discover many more nuggets which will replace anxiety, fears, worries, concerns, and cares with God's peace! Again, this is the core of good Holy Ghost Psychiatry — replacing your thoughts with God's thoughts from His Word!

Exodus 14:13,14

Fear not; stand still (firm, confident, undismayed) and see the salvation of the Lord which He will work for you today. For the Egyptians you have seen today you shall never see again.

The Lord will fight for you, and you shall hold your peace and remain at rest.

Exodus 15:26

If you will diligently hearken to the voice of the Lord your God and will do what is right in His sight, and will listen to and obey His commandments and keep all His statutes, I will put none of the diseases upon you which I brought upon the Egyptians, for *I am the Lord Who heals you.*

Numbers 10:35

Rise up, Lord; let Your enemies be scattered; and let those who hate You flee before You.

Numbers 23:19

God is not a man, that He should tell or act a lie, neither the son of man, that He should feel repentance or compunction [for what He has promised]. Has He said and shall He not do it? Or has He spoken and shall He not make it good?

Deuteronomy 8:18

But you shall [earnestly] remember the Lord your God, for it is He Who gives you power to get wealth, that He may establish His covenant which He swore to your fathers, as it is this day.

(GOD'S ECONOMY NEVER CHANGES, REGARD-LESS OF WHAT HAPPENS IN THE NATURAL!)

Deuteronomy 28:1-14

If you will listen diligently to the voice of the Lord your God, being watchful to do all His commandments which I command you this day, the Lord your God will set you high above all the nations of the earth.

And all these blessings shall come upon you and overtake you if you heed the voice of the Lord your God.

Blessed shall you be in the city and blessed shall you be in the field.

Blessed shall be the fruit of your body and the fruit of your ground and the fruit of your beasts, the increase of your cattle and the young of your flock.

Blessed shall be your basket and your kneading trough.

Blessed shall you be when you come in and blessed shall you be when you go out.

The Lord shall cause your enemies who rise up against you to be defeated before your face; they shall come out against you one way and flee before you seven ways.

The Lord shall command the blessing upon you in your storehouse and in all that you undertake. And He will bless you in the land which the Lord your God gives you.

The Lord will establish you as a people holy to Himself, as He has sworn to you, if you keep the commandments of the Lord your God and walk in His ways.

And all people of the earth shall see that you are called by the name [and in the presence of] the Lord, and they shall be afraid of you.

And the Lord shall make you have a surplus of prosperity, through the fruit of your body, of your livestock, and of your ground, in the land which the Lord swore to your fathers to give you.

The Lord shall open to you His good treasury, the heavens, to give the rain of your land in its season and to bless all the work of your hands; and you shall lend to many nations, but you shall not borrow.

And the Lord shall make you the head, and not the tail: and you shall be above only, and you shall not be beneath, if you heed the commandments of the Lord your God which I command you this day and are watchful to do them.

And you shall not turn aside from any of the words which I command you this day, to the right hand or to the left, to go after other gods to serve them.

Joshua 1:5

No man shall be able to stand before you all the days of your life. As I was with Moses, so I will be with you; I will not fail you or forsake you.

Joshua 1:8

This Book of the Law shall not depart out of your mouth, but you shall meditate on it day and night, that you may observe and do according to all that is written in it. For then you shall make your way prosperous, and then you shall deal wisely and have good success.

2 Chronicles 7:14

If My people, who are called by My name, shall humble themselves, pray, seek, crave, and require of necessity My face and turn from their wicked ways, then will I hear from heaven, forgive their sin, and heal their land.

2 Chronicles 16:9

For the eyes of the Lord run to and fro throughout the whole earth to show Himself strong in behalf of those whose hearts are blameless toward Him.

Psalm 1:1-3

Blessed (happy, fortunate, prosperous, and enviable) is the man who walks and lives not in the counsel of the ungodly [following their advice, their plans and purposes], nor stands [submissive and inactive] in the path where sinners walk, nor sits down [to relax and rest] where the scornful [and the mockers] gather.

But his delight and desire are in the law of the Lord, and on His law (the precepts, the instructions, the teachings of God) he habitually meditates (ponders and studies) by day and by night.

And he shall be like a tree firmly planted [and tended] by the streams of water, ready to bring forth its fruit in its season; its leaf also shall not fade or wither; and everything he does shall prosper [and come to maturity].

Psalm 5:12

For You, Lord, will bless the [uncompromisingly] righteous [him who is upright and in right standing with You]; as with a shield You will surround him with goodwill (pleasure and favor).

Psalm 18:2,3

The Lord is my Rock, my Fortress, and my Deliverer; my God, my keen and firm Strength in Whom I will trust and take refuge, my Shield, and the Horn of my salvation, my High Tower.

I will call upon the Lord, Who is to be praised; so shall I be saved from my enemies.

Psalm 37

Fret not yourself because of evildoers, neither be envious against those who work unrighteousness (that which is not upright or in right standing with God).

For they shall soon be cut down like the grass, and wither as the green herb.

Trust (lean on, rely on, and be confident) in the Lord and do good; so shall you dwell in the land and feed surely on His faithfulness, and truly you shall be fed.

Delight yourself also in the Lord, and He will give you the desires and secret petitions of your heart.

Commit your way to the Lord [roll and repose each care of your load on Him]; trust (lean on, rely on, and be confident) also in Him and He will bring it to pass.

And He will make your uprightness and right standing with God go forth as the light, and your justice and right as [the shining sun of] the noonday.

Be still and rest in the Lord; wait for Him and patiently lean yourself upon Him; fret not yourself because of him who prospers in his way, because of the man who brings wicked devices to pass.

Cease from anger and forsake wrath; fret not yourself — it tends only to evildoing.

For evildoers shall be cut off, but those who wait and hope and look for the Lord [in the end] shall inherit the earth.

For yet a little while, and the evildoers will be no more; though you look with care where they used to be, they will not be found.

But the meek [in the end] shall inherit the earth and shall delight themselves in the abundance of peace.

The wicked plot against the [uncompromisingly] righteous (the upright in right standing with God); they gnash at them with their teeth.

The Lord laughs at [the wicked], for He sees that their own day [of defeat] is coming.

The wicked draw the sword and bend their bows to cast down the poor and needy, to slay those who walk uprightly (blameless in conduct and in conversation).

The swords [of the wicked] shall enter their own hearts, and their bows shall be broken.

Better is the little that the [uncompromisingly] righteous have than the abundance [of possessions] of many who are wrong and wicked.

For the arms of the wicked shall be broken, but the Lord upholds the [consistently] righteous.

The Lord knows the days of the upright and blameless, and their heritage will abide forever.

They shall not be put to shame in the time of evil; and in the days of famine they shall be satisfied.

But the wicked shall perish, and the enemies of the Lord shall be as the fat of lambs [that is consumed in smoke] and as the glory of the pastures. They shall vanish; like smoke shall they consume away.

The wicked borrow and pay not again [for they may be unable], but the [uncompromisingly] righteous deal kindly and give [for they are able].

For such as are blessed of God shall [in the end] inherit the earth, but they that are cursed of Him shall be cut off.

The steps of a [good] man are directed and established by the Lord when He delights in his way [and He busies Himself with his every step].

Though he falls, he shall not be utterly cast down, for the Lord grasps his hand in support and upholds him.

I have been young and now am old, yet have I not seen the [uncompromisingly] righteous forsaken or their seed begging bread.

All day long they are merciful and deal graciously; they lend, and their offspring are blessed.

Depart from evil and do good; and you will dwell forever [securely].

For the Lord delights in justice and forsakes not His saints; they are preserved forever, but the offspring of the wicked [in time] shall be cut off.

[Then] the [consistently] righteous shall inherit the land and dwell upon it forever.

The mouth of the [uncompromisingly] righteous utters wisdom, and his tongue speaks with justice.

The law of his God is in his heart; none of his steps shall slide.

The wicked lie in wait for the [uncompromisingly] righteous and seek to put them to death.

The Lord will not leave them in their hands, or [suffer them to] condemn them when they are judged.

Wait for and expect the Lord and keep and heed His way, and He will exalt you to inherit the land; [in the end] when the wicked are cut off, you shall see it.

I have seen a wicked man in great power and spreading himself like a green tree in its native soil.

Yet he passed away, and behold, he was not; yes, I sought and inquired for him, but he could not be found.

Mark the blameless man and behold the upright, for there is a happy end for the man of peace.

As for transgressors, they shall be destroyed together; in the end the wicked shall be cut off.

But the salvation of the [consistently] righteous is of the Lord; He is their Refuge and secure Stronghold in the time of trouble.

And the Lord helps them and delivers them; He delivers them from the wicked and saves them, because they trust and take refuge in Him.

Psalm 59:1

Deliver me from my enemies, O my God; defend and protect me from those who rise up against me.

Psalm 91

He who dwells in the secret place of the Most High shall remain stable and fixed under the shadow of the Almighty [Whose power no foe can withstand].

I will say of the Lord, He is my Refuge and my Fortress, my God; on Him I lean and rely, and in Him I [confidently] trust!

For [then] He will deliver you from the snare of the fowler and from the deadly pestilence.

[Then] He will cover you with His pinions, and under His wings shall you trust and find refuge; His truth and His faithfulness are a shield and a buckler.

You shall not be afraid of the terror of the night, nor of the arrow (the evil plots and slanders of the wicked) that flies by day.

Nor of the pestilence that stalks in darkness, nor of the destruction and sudden death that surprise and lay waste at noonday.

A thousand may fall at your side, and ten thousand at your right hand, but it shall not come near you.

Only a spectator shall you be [yourself inaccessible in the secret place of the Most High] as you witness the reward of the wicked.

Because you have made the Lord your refuge, and the Most High your dwelling place,

There shall no evil befall you, nor any plague or calamity come near your tent.

For He will give His angels [especial] charge over you to accompany and defend and preserve you in all your ways [of obedience and service].

They shall bear you up on their hands, lest you dash your foot against a stone.

You shall tread upon the lion and adder; the young lion and the serpent shall you trample underfoot.

Because he has set his love upon Me, therefore will I deliver him; I will set him on high, because he knows and understands My name [has a personal knowledge of My mercy, love, and kindness — trusts and relies on Me, knowing I will never forsake him, no, never].

He shall call upon Me, and I will answer him; I will be with him in trouble, I will deliver him and honor him.

With long life will I satisfy him and show him My salvation.

Psalm 92:15

[They are living memorials] to show that the Lord is upright and faithful to His promises; He is my Rock, and there is no unrighteousness in Him.

Psalm 103:1-5

Bless (affectionately, gratefully praise) the Lord, O my soul; and all that is [deepest] within me, bless His holy name!

Bless (affectionately, gratefully praise) the Lord, O my soul, and forget not [one of] all His benefits —

Who forgives [every one of] all your iniquities, Who heals [each one of] all your diseases,

Who redeems your life from the pit and corruption, Who beautifies, dignifies, and crowns you with loving-kindness and tender mercy;

Who satisfies your mouth [your necessity and desire at your personal age and situation] with good so that your youth, renewed, is like the eagle's [strong, overcoming, soaring]!

Psalm 121

I will lift up my eyes to the hills [around Jerusalem, to sacred Mount Zion and Mount Moriah] — From whence shall my help come?

My help comes from the Lord, Who made heaven and earth.

He will not allow your foot to slip or to be moved; He Who keeps you will not slumber.

Behold, He who keeps Israel will neither slumber nor sleep.

The Lord is your keeper; the Lord is your shade on your right hand [the side not carrying a shield].

The sun shall not smite you by day, nor the moon by night.

The Lord will keep you from all evil; He will keep your life.

The Lord will keep your going out and your coming in from this time forth and forevermore.

Psalm 124

If it had not been the Lord Who was on our side—now may Israel say—

If it had not been the Lord Who was on our side when men rose up against us,

Then they would have quickly swallowed us up alive when their wrath was kindled against us;

Then the waters would have overwhelmed us and swept us away, the torrent would have gone over us;

Then the proud waters would have gone over us.

Blessed be the Lord, Who has not given us as prey to their teeth!

We are like a bird escaped from the snare of the fowlers; the snare is broken, and we have escaped!

Our help is in the name of the Lord, Who made heaven and earth.

Proverbs 3:5-8

Lean on, trust in, and be confident in the Lord with all your heart and mind and do not rely on your own insight or understanding.

In all your ways know, recognize, and acknowledge Him, and He will direct and make straight and plain your paths.

Be not wise in your own eyes; reverently fear and worship the Lord and turn [entirely] away from evil.

It shall be health to your nerves and sinews, and marrow and moistening to your bones.

Proverbs 21:30

There is no [human] wisdom or understanding or counsel [that can prevail] against the Lord.

Isaiah 26:3

You will guard him and keep him in perfect and constant peace whose mind [both its inclination and its character] is stayed on You, because he commits himself to You, leans on You, and hopes confidently in You.

Isaiah 41:10-13

Fear not [there is nothing to fear], for I am with you; do not look around you in terror and be dismayed, for I am your God. I will strengthen and harden you to difficulties, yes, I will help you; yes, I will hold you up and retain you with My [victorious] right hand of rightness and justice.

Behold, all they who are enraged and inflamed against you shall be put to shame and confounded; they who strive against you shall be as nothing and shall perish.

You shall seek those who contend with you but shall not find them; they who war against you shall be as nothing, as nothing at all.

For I the Lord your God hold your right hand; I am the Lord, Who says to you, Fear not; I will help you!

Isaiah 43:18,19

Do not [earnestly] remember the former things; neither consider the things of old.

Behold, I am doing a new thing! Now it springs forth; do you not perceive and know it and will you not give heed to it? I will even make a way in the wilderness and rivers in the desert.

Jeremiah 29:11-13

For I know the thoughts and plans that I have for you, says the Lord, thoughts and plans for welfare and peace and not for evil, to give you hope in your final outcome.

Then you will call upon Me, and you will come and pray to Me, and I will hear and heed you.

Then you will seek Me, inquire for, and require Me [as a vital necessity] and find Me when you search for Me with all your heart.

Daniel 11:32

...But the people who know their God shall prove themselves strong and shall stand firm and do exploits [for God].

Joel 2:23-26

Be glad then, you children of Zion, and rejoice in the Lord, your God; for He gives you the former or early rain in just measure and in righteousness, and He causes to come down for you the rain, the former rain and the latter rain, as before.

And the [threshing] floors shall be full of grain and the vats shall overflow with juice [of the grape] and oil.

And I will restore or replace for you the years that the locust has eaten — the hopping locust, the stripping locust, and the crawling locust, My great army which I sent among you.

And you shall eat in plenty and be satisfied and praise the name of the Lord, your God, Who has dealt wondrously with you. And my people shall never be put to shame.

Matthew 8:17

He Himself took [in order to carry away] our weaknesses and infirmities and bore away our diseases.

Matthew 11:28-30

Come to Me, all you who labor and are heavy-laden and overburdened, and I will cause you to rest. [I will ease and relieve and refresh your souls.]

Take My yoke upon you and learn of Me, for I am gentle (meek) and humble (lowly) in heart, and you will find rest (relief and ease and refreshment and recreation and blessed quiet) for your souls.

For My yoke is wholesome (useful, good — not harsh, hard, sharp, or pressing, but comfortable, gracious, and pleasant), and My burden is light and easy to be borne.

Mark 5:36

Overhearing but ignoring what they said, Jesus said to the ruler of the synagogue, Do not be seized with alarm and struck with fear; only keep on believing.

Mark 11:22-26

Have faith in God [constantly].

Truly I tell you, whoever says to this mountain, Be lifted up and thrown into the sea! and does not doubt at all in his heart but believes that what he says will take place, it will be done for him.

For this reason I am telling you, whatever you ask for in prayer, believe (trust and be confident) that it is granted to you, and you will [get it].

And whenever you stand praying, if you have anything against anyone, forgive him and let it drop (leave it, let it go), in order that your Father Who is in heaven may also forgive you your [own] failings and shortcomings and let them drop.

But if you do not forgive, neither will your Father in heaven forgive your failings and shortcomings.

John 10:27

The sheep that are My own hear and are listening to My voice; and I know them, and they follow Me.

John 15:7

If you live in Me [abide vitally united to Me] and My words remain in you and continue to live in your hearts, ask whatever you will, and it shall be done for you.

Romans 8:1

Therefore, [there is] now no condemnation (no adjudging guilty of wrong) for those who are in Christ Jesus, who live [and] walk not after the dictates of the flesh, but after the dictates of the Spirit.

1 Corinthians 2:16

But we have the mind of Christ (the Messiah) and do hold the thoughts (feelings and purposes) of His heart.

Philippians 1:6

And I am convinced and sure of this very thing, that He Who began a good work in you will continue until the day of Jesus Christ [right up to the time of His return], developing [that good work] and perfecting and bringing it to full completion in you.

Philippians 4:6-9

Do not fret or have any anxiety about anything, but in every circumstance and in everything, by prayer and petition (definite requests), with thanksgiving, continue to make your wants known to God.

And God's peace [shall be yours, that tranquil state of a soul assured of its salvation through Christ, and so fearing nothing from God and being content with its earthly lot of whatever sort that is, that peace] which transcends all understanding shall garrison and mount guard over your hearts and minds in Christ Jesus.

For the rest, brethren, whatever is true, whatever is worthy of reverence and is honorable and seemly, whatever is just, whatever is pure, whatever is lovely and lovable, whatever is kind and winsome and gracious, if there is any virtue and excellence, if there is anything worthy of praise, think on and weigh and take account of these things [fix your minds on them].

1 Peter 3:4

But let it be the inward adorning and beauty of the hidden person of the heart, with the incorruptible and unfading charm of a gentle and peaceful spirit, which [is not anxious or wrought up, but] is very precious in the sight of God.

1 Peter 5:7

Casting the whole of your care [all your anxieties, all your worries, all your concerns, once and for all] on Him, for He cares for you affectionately and cares about you watchfully.

3 John 2

Beloved, I pray that you may prosper in every way and [that your body] may keep well, even as [I know] your soul keeps well and prospers.

ABOUT THE AUTHOR

David Crank is a graduate of the Missouri Highway Patrol Academy and was a St. Louis County police officer for five years. He was a juvenile officer for two years. It was while watching a Christian television program that he was born again, and he was filled with the Holy Spirit in a police squad car.

With his wife, Sharon, he began full-time ministry on the evangelistic field, then years later settled in the St. Louis area to build a church and teaching center. Their anointed ministry spans the nation and the world through books, tapes, a radio program, and a television program, "The Message of Maturity." He conducts televised services where people come from all over the United States to receive their healing.

God has opened special doors for David's ministry. He has been interviewed on various Christian television programs such as, "The Believer's Voice of Victory" with Kenneth Copeland, "Richard Roberts Live," "Praise the Lord" on the Trinity Broadcasting Network, and many others.

David ministers in monthly meetings and conferences all across America. He has the innate ability to stir spiritual hunger in the hearts of believers. The cry of his heart is to lift up the name of Jesus and to ascribe to Him all the glory for what He does!

Other Books by David Crank:

Godly Finances and the Bible Way to Pay Off Your Home

Samson: A Type of the Church

Seeking the Lord: The Real Key to Success

Teaching Tapes by David Crank:

Seeking the Lord

Daily Prayer

Having a Passion for God

High- and Low-Grade Spiritual Fellowship

Quench Not, Grieve Not, Resist Not the Holy Spirit

Freedom from Fear, Anxiety, and Panic Attacks

David Crank conducts Holy Spirit and financial seminars across the United States. For information concerning a seminar in your area or to receive a complete book and teaching tape catalog, please write:

David Crank Ministries
1416 Larkin Williams Road
St. Louis, MO 63026
or call
(314) 343-4359

Please feel free to contact the author with your prayer requests and comments.

The Harrison House Vision

Proclaiming the truth and the power
Of the Gospel of Jesus Christ
With excellence;

Challenging Christians to
Live victoriously,
Grow spiritually,
Know God intimately.